Scriptural Rosary

JOHN A. HAMMES, Ph.D.

Our Sunday Visitor Publishing Division
Our Sunday Visitor, Inc.
Huntington, Indiana 46750

Nihil Obstat: Rev. Msgr. Peter A. Dora
Censor Deputatus
Imprimatur: ✠ John Francis Donoghue
Archbishop of Atlanta
September 21, 1998

Most of the citations in this work are taken from the *Douay-Rheims* version of the Bible and some selected passages
from Rev. Stephen J. Hartdegen's *A Chronological Harmony
of the Gospels,* © 1942 by St. Anthony Guild Press. One
citation (Luke 1:78-79) is from the *New American Bible With
Revised New Testament,* © 1986 by the Confraternity of
Christian Doctrine, all rights reserved. Some *Douay-Rheims*
citations have been slightly emended for a number of
reasons, including the editorial decision to conform to
contemporary usage (e.g., Holy Spirit instead of Holy Ghost).
If any copyrighted materials have been inadvertently used in
this work without proper credit being given in one form or
another, please notify Our Sunday Visitor in writing so that
future printings of this work may be corrected accordingly.

ISBN: 0-87973-575-9
LCCCN: 98-67818

Cover design by Monica Watts
PRINTED IN THE UNITED STATES OF AMERICA

Dedicated to my brothers
Burke, Elmore, and Vince —
and their families

Introduction

The Rosary is a beautiful prayer. Time is transcended, as it were, through meditation, and one returns to an age two thousand years ago — to contemplate the life of Our Blessed Lord and Redeemer. Jesus' life, death, and resurrection become events very real to us.

The Rosary devotion, as we have it today, has been practiced in the Church for almost eight hundred years, St. Dominic (+1221) being a significant promoter. The *Our Father* and parts of the *Hail Mary* are taken directly from Scripture. *The Apostles' Creed* dates to early centuries of the Church. In the present work, scriptural passages across the spectrum of the New Testament have been selected for prayerful meditation. The *Douay-Rheims* version of the Bible was used, and passages have been cross-referenced for the convenience of the reader's further study.

In both private and public recitation of the Rosary, I have found that division of each de-

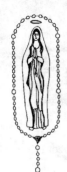

cade into three parts has practical merit for meditation. The *Our Father* may be said after announcement of the mystery. Three *Hail Marys* are then said after the first and second meditative parts of the decade, and four *Hail Marys* said after the last part, together with the *Glory Be to the Father*, and the Fátima prayer given to us by Our Blessed Lady. These prayers may be found at the back of the book. Of course, other meditative arrangements are possible, depending on individual or group preference.

Rosary meditation is meant for all — the young and the aged, the single and the married, the rich and the poor, the educated and the uneducated, the layperson and those professing the religious life. The Rosary is a powerful prayer, sanctioned by Our Blessed Mother at her appearances at Lourdes, Fátima, and in her private revelations to the saints. Through this devotion many favors are received, spiritual and material. Those who pray the Rosary faithfully shall obtain the graces necessary for a virtuous life and final perseverance, as well as other blessings noted in the Rosary promises listed at the end of this volume.

I would like to offer the reader a challenge. Can you set aside fifteen minutes a day? If so, recite the Rosary daily for one month, prayerfully and attentively. You will discover a new love for Our Blessed Lady and her Divine Son, and will be bountifully rewarded.

So, now, find a quiet moment, ask your guardian angel to assist in your meditation, and enter into the mysteries of the divine drama of humanity's redemption and salvation!

One final thing: I want to thank the publishing division of Our Sunday Visitor, Inc. — particularly Jacquelyn Lindsey, Acquisitions Editor, and Henry O'Brien, Managing Editor, Religious Books — for helping to bring this work to fruition.

DAY 1

The First Joyful Mystery

The Angel Gabriel Announces to Mary That She Is to Be the Mother of God

"And in the sixth month, the angel Gabriel was sent from God into a city of Galilee called Nazareth, to a virgin espoused to a man named Joseph, of the house of David; and the virgin's name was Mary" (Lk 1:26-27).

❧~❦~❧

Mary was always submissive to the divine will. On one occasion a woman declared to Jesus: " 'Blessed is the womb that bore thee. . . .' Jesus replied, 'Rather, blessed are they who hear the word of God, and keep it' " (Lk 11:27-28).

❧~❦~❧

According to St. Augustine (+430), Mary's humility was her greatest virtue. Jesus himself said: "Whosoever shalt exalt himself shall be humbled, and he that shall

humble himself shall be exalted" (Mt 23:12; see also Lk 14:11, 18:14).

The Second Joyful Mystery
Mary Visits Her Cousin Elizabeth

The angel Gabriel informs Mary: "And behold thy cousin Elizabeth [has] conceived a son in her old age; and this is the sixth month with her that is called barren, because no word shall be impossible with God" (Lk 1:36-37).

❧∼⁂∼❧

Luke was later to write: "The word of God came to John, the son of Zachary, in the desert. And he came into all the country about the Jordan, preaching the baptism of penance for the remission of sins" (Lk 3:2-3).

❧∼⁂∼❧

"As it is written in the book in the words of Isaiah the prophet, 'A voice of one crying in the wilderness — prepare ye the way of the Lord . . . and all flesh shall see the salvation of God'" (Lk 3:4, 6).

The Third Joyful Mystery
Jesus Is Born in Bethlehem

"And [the shepherds] understood of the word that had been spoken to them concerning this Child. And all they that heard, wondered at those things told them by the shepherds. But Mary kept all these words, pondering them in her heart" (Lk 2:17-19).

❧～❧～❧

"When [the wise men] . . . departed, behold an angel of the Lord appeared in sleep to Joseph, saying, 'Arise, and take the Child and his mother, and fly into Egypt, and be there until I shall tell thee. For it will come to pass that Herod will seek the Child to destroy him' " (Mt 2:13).

❧～❧～❧

"[Joseph] took the Child and his mother by night, and retired into Egypt. And he was there until the death of Herod, that it might be fulfilled which the Lord spoke by the prophet, saying, 'Out of Egypt I have called my Son' " (Mt 2:14-15).

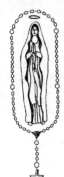

The Fourth Joyful Mystery
The Presentation of Jesus

Jesus speaks to us: "I am the bread of life. Your fathers did eat manna in the desert, and they died. This is the bread descending . . . from heaven, that if anyone eat of it, he may not die" (Jn 6:48-50).

❧∽᷎∽❧

"I am the living bread which came down from heaven. If any man eat of this bread, he shall live forever. And the bread that I will give, is my flesh for the life of the world" (Jn 6:51-52).

❧∽᷎∽❧

"My flesh is [food] indeed, and my blood is drink indeed. He who eats my flesh and drinks my blood, abides in me and I in him" (Jn 6:56-57).

The Fifth Joyful Mystery
Jesus Is Found in the Temple

Even as a boy, Jesus was found in the Temple, going about his Father's business (see Lk 2:49). Later, as a young rabbi in the synagogue, Jesus would cite Isaiah the prophet: "The Spirit of the Lord is upon me. Wherefore he has anointed me to preach the gospel to the poor . . . to heal the contrite of heart" (Lk 4:18).

❧～ॐ～❧

"To preach deliverance to the captives, and sight to the blind; to set at liberty them that are bruised. To preach the acceptable year of the Lord, and the day of reward" (Lk 4:19).

❧～ॐ～❧

"And when he had folded the book, he restored it to the minister, and sat down. And the eyes of all in the synagogue were upon him. [Jesus said] to them, 'This day is fulfilled this Scripture in your [hearing]' " (Lk 4:20-21).

DAY 2

The First Sorrowful Mystery
Our Lord's Agony in the Garden

In speaking of his death, Jesus had once told his disciples: "As Moses lifted up the serpent in the desert, so must the Son of man be lifted up, that whosoever believes in him, may not perish, but have life everlasting" (Jn 3:14-15; see also 8:28, 12:32).

⁂

Earlier, when the disciples wished Jesus to eat, he reminded them: "My [food] is to do the will of him who sent me, that I may perfect his work" (Jn 4:34).

⁂

In contemplating Jesus' fulfillment of his Father's will, let us remember the prayer that he taught us: "Our Father, who art in heaven, hallowed be thy name . . . thy will be done on earth as it is in heaven" (Mt 6:9-10).

The Second Sorrowful Mystery
Our Lord Is Scourged

Jesus exhorts his followers to avoid revenge: "You have heard . . . 'An eye for an eye, a tooth for a tooth.' But I say to you, not to resist evil: . . . if any man strike thee on thy right cheek, turn to him the other also" (Mt 5:38-39; see also Lk 6:29).

❦❧

"You have heard . . . 'Thou shalt love thy neighbor, and hate thy enemy.' But I say to you, love your enemies, do good to them that hate you, and pray for them that persecute and calumniate you" (Mt 5:43-44; see also Lk 6:27-28).

❦❧

Our Savior cautions us: "How narrow is the gate, and straight is the way, which leads to life. And few there are who find it!" (Mt 7:14; see also Lk 13:24).

The Third Sorrowful Mystery
Jesus Is Crowned with Thorns

Jesus, yearning to die for our salvation, said: "And I have a baptism, wherewith I am to be baptized. And how am I straitened until it be accomplished!" (Lk 12:50).

Our Lord told his disciples that they would share in his sufferings: "You shall indeed drink of the chalice that I drink ... and [be baptized] with the baptism wherewith I am baptized" (Mk 10:39).

Our Savior came to redeem us in the eyes of the Father: "The Son of man came not to be administered to, but to minister, and to give his life [as] a redemption for many" (Mt 20:28).

The Fourth Sorrowful Mystery
Jesus Carries the Cross

Jesus speaks to us: "If any man will come after me, let him deny himself, and take up his cross daily, and follow me" (Lk 9:23; see also Mt 16:24, Mk 8:34).

Jesus continues: "For whosoever will save his life, will lose it. And he that shall lose his life for my sake, shall find it" (Mt

16:25; see also Mt 10:39, Mk 8:35, Lk 9:24).

❧～ॐ～❧

"For what doth it profit a man, if he gain the whole world, and lose his own soul? Or what shall a man give in exchange for his soul?" (Mt 16:26; see also Mk 8:36-37, Lk 9:25).

The Fifth Sorrowful Mystery
Our Lord Dies on the Cross

Mary shared the mockery of her Son dying on the cross (see Mt 27:39-40). In the words of Jeremiah the prophet: "All they that passed by the way . . . have hissed, and wagged their heads at the daughter of Jerusalem" (Lam 2:15).

❧～ॐ～❧

"Oh, how sad and sore distressed
Was that Mother highly blessed,
Of that sole-begotten One!"

❧～ॐ～❧

"Christ above in torments hangs
She beneath beholds the pangs,
Of her dying glorious Son!"
— Blessed Jacopone da Todi (+1306)

DAY 3

The First Glorious Mystery
Jesus Rises from the Dead

Jesus had prophesied: " 'Destroy this temple, and in three days I will raise it up' . . . [speaking] of the temple of his body. When, therefore, he had risen from the dead, his disciples remembered that he had said this, and they believed the Scripture, and the word Jesus had said" (Jn 2:19, 21-22).

❧⁓⟡⁓❧

Angels guarded the tomb of Christ. We have been given an angel to guard us in life (see Mt 18:10), one with whom we can converse and develop a personal friendship!

❧⁓⟡⁓❧

Upon his resurrection, as Mark 16:9 tells us, Jesus' first public appearance was to Mary Magdalene. However, many saints believed that he first privately appeared to his Mother.

She, who once had embraced the infant Savior with a mother's love, was now embraced by him in a divine resurrected love.

The Second Glorious Mystery
Jesus Ascends Triumphantly into Heaven

Jesus speaks to us: "Lay not up for yourselves treasures on earth, where the rust, and the moth consume, and where thieves dig through, and steal. But lay up for yourselves treasure in heaven, where neither the rust nor the moth consume, and where thieves do not dig through, nor steal" (Mt 6:19-20; see also Lk 12:33).

❧～✲～❧

While we live on earth, if our treasure be Jesus, our hearts will be in heaven — for he said: "Where thy treasure is, there is thy heart also" (Mt 6:21; see also Lk 12:34).

❧～✲～❧

Jesus taught us to pray: "Our Father, who art in heaven, hallowed be thy name" (Mt 6:9; see also Lk 11:2). So holy is the name of God that the very second commandment mandates its reverence. May we never, never speak that sacred name indifferently or in careless habit.

The Third Glorious Mystery
The Holy Spirit Descends on Mary and the Apostles

"And there appeared to them parted tongues, as it were of fire, and it sat upon each of them. And they were all filled with the Holy Spirit" (Acts 2:3-4).

❧∽◉∽❧

Jesus had earlier said: "I am come to send fire on the earth, and what will I but that it be kindled?" (Lk 12:49).

❧∽◉∽❧

John the Baptist had prophesied: "I indeed baptize you with water. . . . He shall baptize you with the Holy Spirit and with fire" (Mt 3:11). This prophecy was fulfilled when, after his resurrection, Jesus declared to his disciples: "For John indeed baptized with water, but you shall be baptized with the Holy Spirit" (Acts 1:5).

The Fourth Glorious Mystery
Our Blessed Mother Is Assumed into Heaven

From the Canticle of Canticles (Song of Songs), we apply these words to Mary: "I sleep, and my heart watches. The voice of my beloved knocking — Open to me, my sister, my love, my dove, my undefiled" (Cant 5:2).

❧∼⟊∼❧

Mary has been gloriously assumed into heaven. She in whom the Holy Spirit once rested, now rests in the Holy Spirit.

❧∼⟊∼❧

Mary would have us remember the words of her Son: "Be not [anxious] for your life, what you shall eat, nor for your body, what you shall put on. . . . Your Father knows you have need of these things. But seek first the kingdom of God and his justice, and all these things shall be [given] you" (Lk 12:22, 30-31).

The Fifth Glorious Mystery
Mary Is Crowned Queen of Heaven

Mary would have us listen: "He that shall hear me [the Lord God], shall rest without terror, and shall enjoy abundance, without fear of evils" (Prv 1:33).

❧∽♦∽❧

Our Blessed Mother would caution us with these words from Scripture: "Wisdom will not enter into a malicious soul, nor dwell in a body subject to sins. For the Holy Spirit of discipline will flee from the deceitful . . . and shall not abide where iniquity [pervades]" (Wis 1:4-5).

❧∽♦∽❧

"All wisdom is from the Lord God, and has been always with him, and is before all time" (Eccles [Sir] 1:1).

DAY 4

The First Joyful Mystery

The Angel Gabriel Announces to Mary That She Is to Be the Mother of God

The angel Gabriel speaks to Mary: "Fear not, Mary, for thou hast found grace with God. Behold, thou shalt conceive in thy womb and shalt bring forth a Son, and thou shalt call his name, Jesus" (Lk 1:30-31).

❖∼❡∼❖

Paul speaks: "When the fullness of time had come, God sent his Son, made of a woman, made under the law" (Gal 4:4).

❖∼❡∼❖

Mary believed the word of God in the angelic message. Jesus says to us: "Amen, amen, I say to you, he that hears my word, and believes him who sent me, has everlasting life, and . . . is passed from death to life" (Jn 5:24).

The Second Joyful Mystery
Mary Visits Her Cousin Elizabeth

"There was in the days of Herod, the king of Judea, a certain priest named Zachary . . . and his wife . . . Elizabeth. And they were both just before God, walking in all the commandments and justifications of the Lord" (Lk 1:5-6).

❦

"And there appeared to [Zachary] an angel of the Lord. . . . And Zachary, seeing him, was troubled, and fear fell upon him. But the angel said to him, 'Fear not, Zachary, for thy prayer is heard; . . . thy wife, Elizabeth, shall bear thee a son, and thou shalt call his name John" (Lk 1:11-13).

❦

The angel continues: "He shall be great before the Lord; . . . and he shall be filled with the Holy Spirit, even from his mother's womb. And he shall convert many of the children of Israel to the Lord their God" (Lk 1:15-16).

The Third Joyful Mystery

Jesus Is Born in Bethlehem

"And it came to pass, that when they were there, her days were accomplished, that she should be delivered. And she brought forth her firstborn Son, and wrapped him up in swaddling clothes, and laid him in a manger, because there was no room for them in the inn" (Lk 2:6-7).

Jesus speaks: "The foxes have [dens], and the birds of the air nests, but the Son of man has nowhere to lay his head" (Mt 8:20).

Paul writes: "For you know the grace of our Lord Jesus Christ, that being rich, he became poor for your sakes — that through his poverty you might be rich" (2 Cor 8:9).

The Fourth Joyful Mystery
The Presentation of Jesus

In our daily recitation of the Lord's Prayer, we pledge ourselves to praise the name of God, and to work, each in his own way, toward establishing his kingdom on earth (see Mt 6:9-10).

❧∼❦∼❧

In the Lord's Prayer, we request daily bread. In our daily Eucharistic bread, Jesus, we will find spiritual nourishment (see Mt 6:11).

❧∼❦∼❧

In the Lord's Prayer, we beg forgiveness of our sins — a grace given only if we forgive those who have trespassed against us (see Mt 6:12, Lk 11:4). Jesus warned: "If you forgive men their offenses, your heavenly Father will also forgive you your offenses. But if you do not forgive men, neither will your Father forgive you your sins" (Mt 6:14-15).

The Fifth Joyful Mystery
Jesus Is Found in the Temple

The young boy Jesus astounds his listeners with his wisdom. Later he would say: "Whosoever hears my words, and does them, shall be likened to a wise man, who built his house upon rock" (Mt 7:24; see also Lk 6:47-48).

❧∼❦∼❧

"And every one who hears my words, and does them not, shall be like a foolish man, who built his house upon the sand. And the rain fell, and the floods came, and the winds blew, and they beat upon that house, and it fell" (Mt 7:26-27; see also Lk 6:49).

❧∼❦∼❧

Mary's advice at the marriage feast of Cana, where Jesus performed his first miracle at her request, is meant for us as well. There, she instructed the chief steward, "Whatsoever he shall say to you, do" (Jn 2:5).

DAY 5

The First Sorrowful Mystery
Our Lord's Agony in the Garden

In the Lord's Prayer, Jesus teaches us to beseech the Father to deliver us *from* evil (see Mt 6:13). He now permits himself, because of our sins, to be delivered *unto* evil and the "power of darkness" (see Lk 22:53).

❦

Jesus warns us: "From within, out of the heart ... proceed evil thoughts, adulteries, fornications, murders, thefts, covetousness, wickedness, deceit, lasciviousness, an evil eye, blasphemy, pride. ... All these evil things come from within, and defile a man" (Mk 7:21-23). Divine Savior, deliver us from sin!

❦

In time of temptation, may we recall Jesus' words: "Amen, amen, I say to you, whosoever commits sin, is the servant of sin" (Jn 8:34).

The Second Sorrowful Mystery
Our Lord Is Scourged

"And after a while, they that stood by said again to Peter, 'Surely thou art one of them, for thou art also a Galilean.' But he began to curse and to swear, 'I know not this man of whom you speak'" (Mk 14:70-71).

❧～❦～❧

Jesus speaks to us: "Whosoever denies me before men, I will deny before my Father, who is in heaven" (Mt 10:33). Peter repented of his denial of Christ. Shall I repent mine?

❧～❦～❧

Jesus also said: "He that loves father or mother more than me, is not worthy of me, and he that loves son or daughter more than me, is not worthy of me" (Mt 10:37). The very first commandment decrees that love of God must supersede all other love.

The Third Sorrowful Mystery
Jesus Is Crowned with Thorns

"And stripping him, they put a scarlet cloak upon him. And platting a crown of thorns, they put it upon his head, and a reed in his right hand" (Mt 27:28-29; see also Mk 15:17, Jn 19:2).

❖⟊❧⟊❖

On the last day, Jesus' crown will be that of king and judge. He himself declared: "When the Son of man will come in his majesty, and all his angels with him . . . [he] shall say to those on his right hand, 'Come, ye blessed of my father, possess the kingdom prepared for you' . . . [and to those on his left hand] 'Depart from me, ye cursed, into everlasting fire, which was prepared for the devil and his angels' " (Mt 25:31, 34, 41).

❖⟊❧⟊❖

Jesus warns those in danger of hell: "For I was hungry, and you gave me not to eat . . . thirsty, and you gave me not to drink . . . a stranger, and you took me not in . . . naked, and you clothed me not; sick, and in

prison, and you did not visit me"
(Mt 25:42-43).

The Fourth Sorrowful Mystery
Jesus Carries the Cross

As we encounter Jesus on the
way to Calvary, may our plea be that
of the leper who had earlier encoun-
tered him. The evangelist writes:
"And there came a leper [to Jesus],
beseeching him, and kneeling
down, said, 'If thou wilt, thou canst
make me clean.' And Jesus, having compassion on him, stretched forth his hand,
and touching him, said to him, 'I will. Be
thou made clean'" (Mk 1:40-41; see also
Lk 5:12-13).

✤✥∾❦∾✥✤

If we but repent, Jesus will say to
us, as he said to the paralytic: "Be of good
heart, thy sins are forgiven thee" (Mt 9:2).

✤✥∾❦∾✥✤

Jesus extends this divine invitation,
cited by all of the evangelists: "Follow me"
(Mt 9:9, 16:24, 19:21; Mk 2:14, 8:34,
10:21; Lk 5:27, 9:23, 18:22; Jn 1:43,
21:19).

The Fifth Sorrowful Mystery
Our Lord Dies on the Cross

"Now there stood by the cross of Jesus, his mother" (Jn 19:25).

❧∼❦∼❧

"You are indeed fortunate, if at death you are bound with the sweet chains of the love of the Mother of God! They are chains that will ensure your eternal salvation" (St. Alphonsus Liguori, Doctor of the Church, +1787).

❧∼❦∼❧

"O wretched sinner, this great Virgin, who is the Mother of your God and Judge, is also the advocate of the whole human race . . . she refuses no one" (St. Thomas of Villanova, +1555).

DAY 6

The First Glorious Mystery
Jesus Rises from the Dead

Earlier, Jesus had declared to the Samaritan woman at the well: "He that shall drink of the water that I shall give him shall [never thirst]. . . . The water that I shall give . . . shall become in him a fountain of water, springing up into everlasting life" (Jn 4:13-14).

※～❦～※

Also, John writes: "Now, on the last great day of the [feast], Jesus stood and cried out, saying, 'If any man thirst, let him come to me and drink. He that believes, as the Scripture says, "Out of [him] shall flow rivers of living water." ' Now he said this of the Spirit whom they would receive, who believed in him" (Jn 7:37-39).

※～❦～※

We have been washed of our sins by the water of baptism and the blood of Redemption. John observes: "This is he who came

39

by water and blood, Jesus Christ — not in water only, but in water and blood" (1 Jn 5:6).

The Second Glorious Mystery
Jesus Ascends Triumphantly into Heaven

We must work to bring others to heaven with us. Jesus said: "The harvest indeed is great, but the laborers are few. Pray ye, therefore, the Lord of the harvest, that he send laborers into his harvest" (Lk 10:2).

❧⟶❦⟵❧

As Jesus' followers, we must heed the voice of the Magisterium — the successors of Peter and the apostles — for Jesus declared to his apostles: "He who hears you, hears me, and he who despises you, despises me. And he who despises me, despises him who sent me" (Lk 10:16).

❧⟶❦⟵❧

Our secular duties are never to interfere with our obligations to God and his Church. Jesus said: "Render therefore to Caesar the things that are Caesar's, and to God the things that are God's" (Mt 22:21, Mk 12:17, Lk 20:25).

The Third Glorious Mystery
The Holy Spirit Descends on Mary and the Apostles

Our Savior declared to Nicodemus: "Amen, amen, I say unto thee, unless a man be born again of water and the Holy Spirit, he cannot enter the kingdom of God" (Jn 3:5).

❧∽☙∽❧

We must transcend the flesh in order to receive the Spirit. Jesus stated: "That which is born of the flesh, is flesh, and that which is born of the Spirit, is spirit" (Jn 3:6).

❧∽☙∽❧

The Spirit will liberate us. Jesus said: "The Spirit breathes where he wills, and you hear his voice, but you know not whence he comes or where he goes. So is everyone that is born of the Spirit" (Jn 3:8).

41

The Fourth Glorious Mystery
Our Blessed Mother Is Assumed into Heaven

"Behold holy Mary in glory, the Mother of the Lord, exuberant with joy! She is the peak and model of virginity; she is the mother of everything holy and incorrupt" (St. Leander of Seville, +600).

❧∾℘∾❧

Paul's words on love describe that virtue in our Blessed Lady: "Love is patient, is kind; love envies not, deals not perversely, is not puffed up, is not ambitious . . . is not provoked to anger, thinks no evil" (1 Cor 13:4-5).

❧∾℘∾❧

"[Love] rejoices not in iniquity, but rejoices with the truth. [Love] bears all things . . . endures all things. . . . And now there remain faith, hope, and love . . . but the greatest of these is love" (1 Cor 13:6-7, 13).

The Fifth Glorious Mystery
Mary Is Crowned Queen of Heaven

"The Blessed Virgin, who was equal to and even more superior in merit to all men and angels, was exalted above the celestial orders" (St. Thomas Aquinas, Doctor of the Church, +1274).

❦❧

Our Lady would have us heed Paul's words: "Rejoice in the Lord always; again I say, rejoice! . . . [Be not anxious,] but in everything by prayer and supplication, with thanksgiving, let your petitions be known to God. And [may] the peace of God, which surpasses all understanding, keep your hearts and minds in Christ Jesus" (Phil 4:4-7).

❦❧

On our deathbed, may we be able to say with Paul: "I have fought a good fight, I have finished my course, I have kept the faith. For the rest, there is laid up for me a crown of justice, which the Lord, the just judge, will render to me at that day; and not only to me, but to those also who love his coming" (2 Tm 4:7-8).

43

DAY 7

The First Joyful Mystery

The Angel Gabriel Announces to Mary That She Is to Be the Mother of God

The angel Gabriel informs Mary: "He shall be great, and shall be called the Son of the Most High, and the Lord God will give unto him the throne of David, his father; and he shall reign in the house of Jacob forever, and of his kingdom there shall be no end" (Lk 1:32-33).

❧～❦～❧

Jesus expresses his love for those of his kingdom: "Blessed are the poor in spirit, for theirs is the kingdom of heaven. Blessed are the meek, for they shall possess the land. Blessed are they who mourn, for they shall be comforted" (Mt 5:3-5; see also Lk 6:20).

❧～❦～❧

"Blessed are they who hunger and thirst after justice, for they shall be filled. . . . Blessed are the clean of heart, for they

45

shall see God. Blessed are the peacemakers, for they shall be called the children of God" (Mt 5:6-9; see also Lk 6:21).

The Second Joyful Mystery
Mary Visits Her Cousin Elizabeth

Zachary questions the angel regarding his and Elizabeth's future child: " 'Whereby shall I know this? For I am an old man, and my wife is advanced in years.' And the angel . . . said to him, 'I am Gabriel, who stand before God, and am sent to speak to thee, and to bring thee these good tidings' " (Lk 1:18-19).

Gabriel punishes Zachary for his lack of faith in God's message: "And behold, thou shalt be dumb, and shalt not be able to speak until the day wherein these things shall come to pass, because thou hast not believed my words, which shall be fulfilled in their time" (Lk 1:20).

Later, Zachary is healed: "And they made signs to his father, how he would have [his son] called. And ... he wrote, saying, 'John is his name.' And immediately his mouth was opened, and his tongue loosed, and he spoke, blessing God" (Lk 1:62-64).

The Third Joyful Mystery
Jesus Is Born in Bethlehem

"And there were in the same country shepherds watching ... over their flock. And behold, an angel of the Lord stood by them, and the brightness of God shone round about them" (Lk 2:8-9).

❧～ᵒ～❧

Jesus would later say: "I am the light of the world. He who follows me walks not in darkness, but shall have the light of life" (Jn 8:12).

❧～ᵒ～❧

After his cure of the blind man, Jesus declared: "As long as I am in the world, I am the light of the world" (Jn 9:5). He remains with us, in the most Blessed Sacrament of

the Eucharist, to be our light on our pilgrimage of faith.

The Fourth Joyful Mystery
The Presentation of Jesus

Simeon praises God: "Now . . . dismiss thy servant, O Lord, according to thy word, in peace, because my eyes have seen thy salvation, which thou hast prepared before the face of all people" (Lk 2:29-31).

In future, Jesus' listeners would say: "We ourselves have heard him, and know that this is indeed the Savior of the world" (Jn 4:42).

When treated unjustly and rejected, let us remember Jesus' words: "Blessed are they who suffer persecution for justice' sake, for theirs is the kingdom of heaven" (Mt 5:10).

The Fifth Joyful Mystery
Jesus Is Found in the Temple

Even as a youth, our Savior was impressive with his divine enlightenment. Luke writes that when Jesus was found in the Temple "all who heard him were astonished at his wisdom and his answers" (Lk 2:47).

※～～～※

Later, Jesus would say to those who followed him: "You are the salt of the earth. But if the salt lose its savor, with what shall it be salted? It is then good for nothing, but to be cast out, and to be trodden upon by men" (Mt 5:13).

※～～～※

"You are the light of the world. . . . Let your light shine before men, that they may see your good works, and glorify your Father who is in heaven" (Mt 5:14, 16).

DAY 8

The First Sorrowful Mystery
Our Lord's Agony in the Garden

"Then Jesus came with them to a country place, which is called Gethsemane, and he said to his disciples, 'Sit . . . here, till I go [over there] to pray.' And taking with him Peter, and the two sons of Zebedee, he began to grow sorrowful and to be sad" (Mt 26:36-37; see also Mk 14:32-33).

❧❀❧

Jesus on other occasions mourned humanity's sin. For example, Luke writes that "when [Jesus] drew near, seeing the city [of Jerusalem], he wept over it" (Lk 19:41).

❧❀❧

At another time, Luke tells of Jesus' lament: "Jerusalem, Jerusalem, that killest the prophets, and stonest them who are sent to thee, how often would I have gathered thy children, as the bird her brood

under her wings, and thou wouldst not!" (Lk 13:34; see also Mt 23:37).

The Second Sorrowful Mystery
Our Lord Is Scourged

"Pilate, therefore, went into the hall again, and called Jesus, and said to him, 'Art thou the king of the Jews?' . . . Jesus answered, 'My kingdom is not of this world' " (Jn 18:33, 36; see also Mt 27:11, Mk 15:2, Lk 23:3).

✣

Jesus had earlier said to his apostles: "You have continued with me. . . . And I appoint to you, as the Father has appointed to me, a kingdom" (Lk 22:28-29).

✣

Paul warns that only the virtuous shall enter God's kingdom: "Know you this, and understand, that no fornicator, nor unclean, nor covetous person . . . has any inheritance in the kingdom of Christ, and of God" (Eph 5:5).

The Third Sorrowful Mystery

Jesus Is Crowned with Thorns

Do we really love Jesus? He tells us:
"If you love me, keep my commandments"
(Jn 14:15).

＊✿＊

Let us ask of Mary:
"O thou Mother, fount of love
Touch my spirit from above,
Make my heart with thine accord."

＊✿＊

"Make me feel as thou hast felt,
Make my soul to glow and melt,
With the love of Christ my Lord!"
— Blessed Jacopone da Todi (+1306)

The Fourth Sorrowful Mystery
Jesus Carries the Cross

"And there followed him a great multitude of people and of women, who bewailed and lamented him. But Jesus, turning to them, said, 'Daughters of Jerusalem, weep not over me, but weep for yourselves, and for your children'" (Lk 23:27-28).

❦

We should be fearful of the Last Judgment. Jesus said: "And immediately after the tribulation of those days, the sun shall be darkened, and the moon shall not give her light, and the stars shall fall from heaven, and the powers of the heavens shall be moved" (Mt 24:29; see also Mk 13:24-25, Lk 21:25-26).

❦

Jesus continues: "And then shall appear the sign of the Son of man in heaven, and . . . all the tribes of the earth [shall] mourn. And they shall see the Son of man coming in the clouds of heaven with great power and majesty" (Mt 24:30; see also Mk 13:26, Lk 21:27).

54

The Fifth Sorrowful Mystery
Our Lord Dies on the Cross

"Jesus again [cried out] with a loud voice . . . and bowing his head, gave up [his spirit]" (Mt 27:50; see also Jn 19:30).

❧～ℯ～❧

We empathize with Jesus' mother:
"Bruised, derided, cursed, defiled,
She beheld her tender Child
All with bloody scourges rent."

❧～ℯ～❧

"For the sins of his own nation,
Saw Him hang in desolation,
Till His spirit forth he sent."
— Blessed Jacopone da Todi (+1306)

DAY 9

The First Glorious Mystery
Jesus Rises from the Dead

Jesus promises us: "Amen, amen, I say to you — if any man keep my word, he shall not see death forever" (Jn 8:51).

❧~❦~❧

Our Divine Savior assures his grace and strength: "Ask, and it shall be given you; seek, and you shall find; knock, and it shall be opened to you" (Mt 7:7, Lk 11:9).

❧~❦~❧

"Many other signs Jesus also did in the sight of his disciples, which are not written in this book. But these are written that you may believe that Jesus is the Christ, the Son of God. And that believing, you may have life in his name" (Jn 20:30-31).

The Second Glorious Mystery
Jesus Ascends Triumphantly into Heaven

"While they looked on, [Jesus] was raised up, and a cloud received him out of their sight. And [while] they were beholding him going up to heaven, two men stood by them in white garments, who . . . said, 'Ye men of Galilee, why stand you looking up to heaven? This Jesus, who is taken up from you into heaven . . . shall come as you have seen him go . . .' " (Acts 1:9-11).

❧❀❀❧

Daniel the prophet had written some two hundred years earlier: "I beheld therefore in the vision of the night . . . one like the Son of man [coming] with the clouds of heaven" (Dan 7:13).

❧❀❀❧

Paul writes of the Father exalting Christ above the angels: "[God] . . . raising him up from the dead, and setting him at his right hand, in the heavenly places, above all principality, and power, and virtue, and dominion, and every name that is named, not only in this world, but also in that which is to come" (Eph 1:20-21).

The Third Glorious Mystery
The Holy Spirit Descends on Mary and the Apostles

We must prepare our souls in order to receive gifts of the Holy Spirit. Christ said: "No man puts new wine into old [wineskins]; otherwise the new wine will burst the [wineskins], and it will be spilled, . . . But new wine must be put into new [wineskins]" (Lk 5:37-38; see also Mt 9:17, Mk 2:22).

༺~ྀ~༻

We should be open to the Holy Spirit — as he speaks through the Magisterium — lest Jesus say of us: "This people honors me with their lips, but their heart is far from me. And in vain do they worship me, teaching doctrines and commandments of men" (Mt 15:8-9, Mk 7:6-7).

༺~ྀ~༻

Jesus warns: "Whosoever shall be ashamed of me, and of my words, in this adulterous and sinful generation, [of him] the Son

of man also shall be ashamed, when he shall come in the glory of the Father, with the holy angels" (Mk 8:38; see also Lk 9:26).

The Fourth Glorious Mystery
Our Blessed Mother Is Assumed into Heaven

"I hold that Mary is in Christ and with Christ — in Christ, because in him we live and move and have our being [Acts 17:28]; with Christ, because she is assumed into glory" (St. Augustine, Father and Doctor of the Church, +430).

❧⸱⟶ℓ⟶⸱❧

Mary would affirm Paul's petition: "May the God of peace . . . make you perfect in every good work, that you may do his will, working in you that which is well pleasing in his sight, through Jesus Christ, to whom is glory for ever and ever" (Heb 13:20-21).

❧⸱⟶ℓ⟶⸱❧

With Mary — and in the words of Peter — let us praise God: "Blessed be the God and Father of our Lord Jesus Christ,

who according to his great mercy has re-
generated us unto a lively hope, through
the resurrection of Jesus Christ from the
dead" (1 Pt 1:3).

The Fifth Glorious Mystery
Mary Is Crowned Queen of Heaven

"We truly confess Mary to be Queen
of Heaven, because she brought forth the
King of Angels!" (St. Augustine, Father and
Doctor of the Church, +430).

❧～❦～❧

Before joining Mary and her Divine
Son, we must first fulfill our mission on
earth. Peter writes: "Be you also as living
stones . . . a spiritual house, a holy priesthood, to offer up spiritual sacrifices, acceptable to God by Jesus Christ" (1 Pt 2:5).

❧～❦～❧

Peter continues: "You are a chosen
generation, a royal priesthood, a holy nation, a chosen people, that you may declare his virtues, who has called you out
of darkness into his admirable
light" (1 Pt 2:9).

DAY 10

The First Joyful Mystery

The Angel Gabriel Announces to Mary That She Is to Be the Mother of God

"And Mary said to the angel, 'How shall this be done, because I know not man?' And the angel answering, said to her, 'The Holy Spirit shall come upon thee, and the power of the Most High shall over-shadow thee. And therefore, the Holy [One] . . . born of thee shall be called the Son of God' " (Lk 1:34-35).

❧⟿❦⟿❧

As the Son of God, Jesus shares his Father's divinity. He said to his apostles: "Have I been so long a time with you, and you have not known me? Philip, he who sees me, sees the Father also" (Jn 14:9).

❧⟿❦⟿❧

"If I seek the Mother, I see that she is a Virgin. If I seek the Virgin, I see that she is a Mother. And this virginity is ever incor-

rupt, ever perfect, ever inviolate" (St. Ildephonsus, +667).

The Second Joyful Mystery
Mary Visits Her Cousin Elizabeth

Mary praises God: "And his mercy is from generation unto generations, to those who fear him" (Lk 1:50).

❧∽ॐ∽❧

Our Lord, as the evangelist tells us, bestows his mercy on all: "And Jesus went about Galilee, teaching in their synagogues, and preaching the gospel of the kingdom, and healing all diseases and infirmities among the people" (Mt 4:23).

❧∽ॐ∽❧

Jesus speaks to suffering humanity: "I [have] come that they may have life, and may have it more abundantly" (Jn 10:10).

The Third Joyful Mystery
Jesus Is Born in Bethlehem

"And the angel said to them, 'Fear not, for behold, I bring you tidings of great joy, that shall be to all the people. For this day is born to you a Savior, who is Christ, the Lord, in the city of David. And this shall be a sign to you — you shall find the infant wrapped in swaddling clothes, and laid in a manger'" (Lk 2:10-12).

❧∽ᏇᏇ∽❧

We are given the tidings of the joy of Christ. Paul writes: "[May] the God of hope fill you with all joy and peace in believing — that you may abound in hope, and in the power of the Holy Spirit" (Rom 15:13).

❧∽ᏇᏇ∽❧

With Christ we can bear suffering with joy. Paul prays that we "may walk worthy of God, in all things pleasing, being fruitful in every good work, and increasing in the knowledge of God — strengthened with all might, according to the power of his glory, in all patience and long-suffering with joy" (Col 1:10-11).

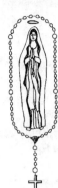

The Fourth Joyful Mystery
The Presentation of Jesus

"And Simeon blessed them, and said to Mary, his mother, 'Behold, this child is set for the ruin, and for the [rise] of many in Israel, and for a sign that shall be contradicted' " (Lk 2:34).

❧～❦～❧

Jesus came to raise us, physically and spiritually. Compassionately, he said: "They who are in health need not a physician, but they who are sick" (Mt 9:12).

❧～❦～❧

Our Lord expects all of us, with his grace, to become saints — faithful images of the divine: "Be you therefore perfect, [just as] your heavenly Father is perfect" (Mt 5:48).

The Fifth Joyful Mystery
Jesus Is Found in the Temple

"And his mother said to him, 'Son, why hast thou done so to us? Behold, thy father and I have sought thee, sorrowing' " (Lk 2:48).

✦∾ℰ∾✦

Though sinless, Mary and Joseph experience the sorrow of that sinful soul who has lost God. Words of Jeremiah the prophet reflect their suffering: "My sorrow is above sorrow, my heart mourns within me" (Jer 8:18).

✦∾ℰ∾✦

When we have lost Jesus, let us turn to him, as did the blind beggar, and beseech him: "Jesus, Son of David, have mercy on me" (Lk 18:38, Mk 10:47; see also Mt 20:30).

DAY 11

The First Sorrowful Mystery
Our Lord's Agony in the Garden

"Then he said to them, 'My soul is sorrowful unto death. Stay you here, and watch with me'" (Mt 26:38, Mk 14:34).

❦

To be Christ's follower is to be detached from material possessions and to give to those less fortunate. Jesus said to the rich young man: "If thou wilt be perfect, go sell what thou hast and give to the poor, and thou shalt have treasure in heaven — and come, follow me" (Mt 19:21; see also Mk 10:21, Lk 18:22).

❦

The young man sorrowfully departed, for he had great wealth. Jesus said to his disciples: "It is easier for a camel to pass through an eye of a needle, than for a rich man to enter the kingdom of heaven" (Mt 19:24; see also Mk 10:23-25, Lk 18:24-25).

The Second Sorrowful Mystery
Our Lord Is Scourged

Pilate asked the crowd: "What shall I do then with Jesus, who is called Christ? They [answered]: Let him be crucified" (Mt 27:22-23; see also Mk 15:12-13, Lk 23:20-21).

❧⦿❧

"The Jews sought the more to kill [Jesus], because he did not only break the sabbath, but also said that God was his Father, making himself equal to God" (Jn 5:18).

❧⦿❧

Let us have the faith of the blind man, whom Jesus healed and then asked: " 'Dost thou believe in the Son of God?' He answered, 'Who is he, Lord, that I may believe in him?' And Jesus said to him, 'Thou hast both seen him, and it is he who [speaks] with thee.' And he said, 'I believe, Lord.' And falling down, he adored him" (Jn 9:35-38).

The Third Sorrowful Mystery
Jesus Is Crowned with Thorns

"And spitting on him, they took the reed, and struck him on the head" (Mt 27:30; see also Mk 15:19).

❧～✤～❧

Our sins of impurity are the spittle upon Christ's countenance. Paul writes: "This is the will of God — your sanctification; . . . that every one of you should know how to possess his [body] in sanctification and honor, not in the passion of lust, like the Gentiles, who know not God" (1 Thess 4:3-5).

❧～✤～❧

We should be watchful of temptation. Jesus said: "The light of thy body is thy eye. If thy eye be [sound], thy whole body will be [full of light]. But if thy eye be evil, thy whole body shall be [full of darkness]" (Mt 6:22-23; see also Lk 11:34).

The Fourth Sorrowful Mystery
Jesus Carries the Cross

"And bearing his own cross, he went forth to that place which is called Calvary" (Jn 19:17).

❦❦❦

Jesus assists us in carrying our cross: "Come to me, all you who labor, and are heavy laden, and I will give you rest. Take up my yoke upon you, and learn of me, because I am meek and humble of heart — and you shall find rest for your souls. For my yoke is sweet, and my burden light" (Mt 11:28-30).

❦❦❦

Our Savior willingly died for us: "I lay down my life, that I may take it up again. No man takes it away from me. . . . I have power to lay it down, and I have power to take it up again" (Jn 10:17-18).

The Fifth Sorrowful Mystery
Our Lord Dies on the Cross

"Now the centurion, and they who were with him, watching Jesus, having seen the earthquake and the things that were done, were greatly afraid, saying, 'Indeed this was the Son of God' " (Mt 27:54; see also Mk 15:39).

❧~෴~❧

Even the devils recognized Jesus' divinity and would cry out: "What have we to do with thee, Jesus, Son of God? Art thou come . . . to torment us before the time?" (Mt 8:29; see also Mk 5:7, Lk 8:28).

❧~෴~❧

"They left all, and followed him" (Lk 5:11; see also Mt 4:20, Mk 1:18). Let us leave all at the foot of the Cross — and follow our Divine Savior!

DAY 12

The First Glorious Mystery
Jesus Rises from the Dead

Jesus had prophesied: "For as Jonah was in the [whale] three days and three nights, so shall the Son of man be in the earth three days and three nights" (Mt 12:40).

❧⚘❧

Our Divine Savior speaks: "As the Father raises up the dead, and gives life, so the Son also gives life to whom he will" (Jn 5:21).

❧⚘❧

Our Lord had told his followers: "Yet a little while, the light is among you. Walk while you have the light, that the darkness [not] overtake you. . . . He who walks in darkness knows not where he goes. While you have the light, believe in the light, that you may be children of the light" (Jn 12:35-36).

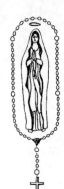

The Second Glorious Mystery
Jesus Ascends Triumphantly into Heaven

If we are to join Christ in heaven, we must first fulfill his work on earth. Otherwise, Jesus warns us: "The kingdom of God shall be taken from you, and shall be given to [those] who bring forth the fruits thereof" (Mt 21:43). In another context, Our Lord said that the unprofitable servant would be cast forth into darkness, where there "shall be weeping and gnashing of teeth" (Mt 25:30).

※～ᔅ～※

Though the road to heaven is difficult, those who persevere in grace shall succeed. Jesus said: "Many are called, but few are chosen" (Mt 22:14).

※～ᔅ～※

Our Divine Savior encourages us: "As the Father has loved me, I also have loved you. Remain in my love! If you keep my commandments, you will remain in my love" (Jn 15:9-10).

The Third Glorious Mystery
The Holy Spirit Descends on Mary and the Apostles

In the power of the Holy Spirit, Peter converted three thousand souls on Pentecost day. The evangelists relate his earlier confession of faith. To Jesus' question, Peter replied: " 'Thou art Christ, the Son of the living God!' And Jesus . . . said to him, 'Blessed art thou, Simon Bar-Jona, because flesh and blood has not revealed it to thee, but my Father, who is in heaven' " (Mt 16:16-17; see also Mk 8:29, Lk 9:20).

❧∼❦∼❧

Jesus then chose Peter to be his vicar on earth: "And I say to thee — thou art Peter, and upon this rock I shall build my church, and the gates of hell shall not prevail against it" (Mt 16:18).

❧∼❦∼❧

Our Divine Savior gave Peter, and his successors, a share in divine authority: "I will give to thee the keys of the kingdom of heaven. And whatsoever thou shalt bind upon earth, shall be bound in heaven . . .

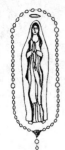

whatsoever thou shalt loose upon earth, it shall be loosed also in heaven" (Mt 16:19).

The Fourth Glorious Mystery
Our Blessed Mother Is Assumed into Heaven

"Mary, the glorious Mother of Christ, was taken up into Heaven by the Lord, while the angelic choirs sang hymns of joy!" (St. Gregory of Tours, +594).

❧∼❦∼❧

Mary would have us heed Peter's words: "If any man speak, let him speak as the words of God; if any man minister, let it be as from the power which God administers. That in all things God may be honored through Jesus Christ — to whom is glory, and dominion, for ever and ever" (1 Pt 4:11).

❧∼❦∼❧

"Rejoice, being partakers of the sufferings of Christ, that when his glory shall be revealed, you may also be glad with exceeding joy" (1 Pt 4:13).

The Fifth Glorious Mystery
Mary Is Crowned Queen of Heaven

"Even when the Mother of God lived in this valley of tears, she was inexpressibly loving and merciful toward the afflicted. How much more compassionate is she now since she reigns happily in heaven!" (St. Bonaventure, Doctor of the Church, +1274).

❧❧❧

According to St. Augustine and St. Jerome, Mary's humility was her crowning virtue. Peter speaks: " 'God resists the proud, and gives grace to the humble.' . . . Cast all your [troubles] upon him, for he [cares] for you" (1 Pt 5:5-7).

❧❧❧

While on earth, we are cautioned by Peter: "Be sober, and watch, because your adversary, the devil, as a roaring lion, goes about, seeking whom he may devour" (1 Pt 5:8). If, when tempted, we fly to Mary, she will protect us from Satan.

DAY 13

The First Joyful Mystery

The Angel Gabriel Announces to Mary That She Is to Be the Mother of God

"Now the birth of Christ was thus: When Mary, his mother, was espoused to Joseph, before they came together, she was found with child by the Holy Spirit" (Mt 1:18).

༺∾་ཕ་∾༻

Matthew cites Isaiah the prophet: "[Those] who walked in darkness have seen a great light. To those who dwelt in the region of the shadow of death, light has risen" (Mt 4:16; see also Is 9:2).

༺∾་ཕ་∾༻

We should imitate the humility of Mary and Joseph: "Be humble in the sight of the Lord, and he will exalt you" (Jas 4:10).

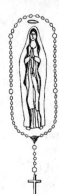

The Second Joyful Mystery
Mary Visits Her Cousin Elizabeth

Mary praises God: "He has filled the hungry with good things, and the rich he has sent away empty. He has received Israel his servant, being mindful of his mercy. As he spoke to our fathers, to Abraham, and to his seed forever" (Lk 1:53-55).

❧⤝⚬ᵹᵕᗢ⤞❧

We exult with the Psalmist: "Give glory to him! Praise you his name. For the Lord is sweet. His mercy endures forever, and his truth to generation and generation" (Ps 99:4-5).

❧⤝⚬ᵹᵕᗢ⤞❧

The words of the archangel Raphael to Tobit confirm such praise: "Bless . . . the God of heaven, give glory to him in the sight of all who live, because he has shown his mercy to you" (Tob 12:6).

The Third Joyful Mystery
Jesus Is Born in Bethlehem

The prophet Isaiah speaks: "Drop down dew, ye heavens, from above, and let the clouds rain [on] the just. Let the earth be opened, and bud forth a savior" (Is 45:8).

※～◌～※

"Be you, therefore, also patient, and strengthen your hearts — for the coming of the Lord draws near" (Jas 5:8).

※～◌～※

We say with David the prophet: "The Lord is my rock, and my strength, and my savior. . . . I will call on the Lord, who is worthy to be praised, and I shall be saved from my enemies" (2 Kgs 22:2, 4).

The Fourth Joyful Mystery
The Presentation of Jesus

Simeon prophesies to Mary: "And thy own soul a sword shall pierce, that out of many hearts thoughts may be revealed" (Lk 2:35).

※～◌～※

We apply these words from Jeremiah the prophet to Mary: "I sigh, and there is none to comfort me . . . my sighs are many, and my heart is sorrowful" (Lam 1:21-22).

※～◌～※

Contemplating her Son's future death, Mary's soul was in continual anguish. As the prophet wrote: "I will be mindful and remember, and my soul shall languish within me" (Lam 3:20).

The Fifth Joyful Mystery
Jesus Is Found in the Temple

"And [Jesus] said to them, 'How is it that you sought me? Did you not know that I must be about the things that are my Father's?' " (Lk 2:49).

❧⁓❦⁓❧

The Father would later verify Jesus' mission: "A bright cloud overshadowed them, and behold, a voice [came] out of the cloud, saying, 'This is my beloved Son, in whom I am well pleased. Hear ye him' " (Mt 17:5; see also Mk 9:6, Lk 9:34-35).

❧⁓❦⁓❧

Jesus always implemented his Father's will. He announced: "I seek not my own will, but the will of him who sent me" (Jn 5:30).

The First Sorrowful Mystery
Our Lord's Agony in the Garden

"And going a little farther, he fell upon his face, praying, and saying, 'O my Father, if it is possible, let this chalice pass from me. Nevertheless, not as I will, but as thou wilt' " (Mt 26:39; see also Mk 14:35-36, Lk 22:41-42).

❧∼❦∼❧

We too must fulfill the divine will. Jesus said: "Not every one who says to me, 'Lord, Lord,' shall enter into the kingdom of heaven. But he who does the will of my Father, who is in heaven ... shall enter into the kingdom of heaven" (Mt 7:21).

❧∼❦∼❧

In obeying the Father, we enter into an intimate relationship with Christ, who declared: "Whosoever shall do the will of my Father, who is in heaven, ... is my brother, and

sister, and mother" (Mt 12:50; see also Mk 3:35, Lk 8:21).

The Second Sorrowful Mystery
Our Lord Is Scourged

Jesus, being divine, foresaw our repentance for sin, and was thereby comforted. He had declared: "I say to you ... there shall be joy in heaven [over] one sinner who does penance, more than [over] ninety-nine just who need not penance" (Lk 15:7).

❧～◌～❧

We are all prodigal children, having wasted our lives in sin. If we repent and return to the Father, Jesus said, he will see us approaching, and with compassion and love run to meet us. He will kiss us with pardon and mercy, and bring us safely into his heavenly kingdom (see Lk 15:20).

❧～◌～❧

Our Divine Savior, having pity on us, promises: "The Son of man [has] come to seek, and to save that which was lost" (Lk 19:10).

The Third Sorrowful Mystery
Jesus Is Crowned with Thorns

Our Lord warns us of Satan: "He was a murderer from the beginning, and he abides not in the truth, because truth is not in him. . . . He is a liar, and the father thereof" (Jn 8:44).

❧❧❦❧❧

May these words, addressed by Jesus to his enemies, never be spoken to us: "He that is of God, hears the words of God. Therefore, you hear them not, because you are not of God" (Jn 8:47).

❧❧❦❧❧

In following Jesus, we shall possess the truth, for he said: "If you continue in my word, you shall be my disciples indeed. And you shall know the truth, and the truth shall make you free" (Jn 8:31-32).

The Fourth Sorrowful Mystery
Jesus Carries the Cross

"And when they had come to the place which is called Calvary, they crucified him there . . . [along with two] robbers, one on the right hand, and one on the left. And Jesus said, 'Father, forgive them, for they know not what they do'" (Lk 23:33-34).

❧~❦~❧

We are to follow Jesus' example of forgiveness. He tells us: "If you forgive men their offenses, your heavenly Father will also forgive you your offenses. But if you will not forgive men, neither will your Father forgive you your sins" (Mt 6:14-15).

❧~❦~❧

We should forgive others while there is time. Jesus warns us: "Wherefore, be ready because at [the] hour you know not, the Son of man will come" (Mt 24:44).

The Fifth Sorrowful Mystery

Our Lord Dies on the Cross

Caiphas, the high priest, unwittingly prophesied our redemption. Earlier, he had said to the council: "Neither do you consider that it is expedient for you that one man should die for the people, [lest] the whole nation perish" (Jn 11:50).

❦

In the parable of the vineyard keepers, Jesus had spoken of the Father's love for us: "Then the lord of the vineyard said, 'What shall I do? I will send my beloved son . . . [perhaps] when they see him, they will reverence him'" (Lk 20:13; see also Mt 21:37, Mk 12:6).

❦

But we, through sin, have rejected that Son: "And laying hold on him, they killed him, and cast him out of the vineyard" (Mk 12:8; see also Mt 21:39, Lk 20:15).

DAY 15

The First Glorious Mystery
Jesus Rises from the Dead

Our Lord taught us to pray: "Our Father, who art in heaven, hallowed be thy name" (Mt 6:9). Jesus is now with the Father in heaven, gloriously reigning, and our hope is to be someday with them, and the Holy Spirit, forever!

❧∾⸎∽❧

What we treasure determines our deeds. Jesus said: "A good man out of a good treasure brings forth good things, and an evil man out of an evil treasure brings forth evil things" (Mt 12:35).

❧∾⸎∽❧

We should be more concerned about our suffering fellow humans than in pleasing friends. Jesus declared: "When thou makest a dinner or a supper, call not thy friends, nor thy brethren. . . . But [instead] . . . call the poor, the feeble, the lame, and the blind. And thou shalt be blessed . . . for

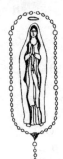

recompense shall be made thee at the resurrection of the just" (Lk 14:12-14).

The Second Glorious Mystery
Jesus Ascends Triumphantly into Heaven

Jesus desires us to be part of him: "I am the vine, you the branches. He who abides in me and I in him, the same bears much fruit — for without me you can do nothing" (Jn 15:5).

❧～❦～❧

May our lives be such that Jesus will say to us, as he did to his apostles: "You are my friends, if you do the things that I command you. I will not now call you servants, for the servant knows not what his lord does. But I have called you friends, because all things whatsoever I have heard from the Father, I have made known to you" (Jn 15:14-15).

❧～❦～❧

In a certain sense, Jesus' words to his apostles are applicable to us: "You have not chosen me, but I have chosen you, and appointed you, that you should go, and should bring forth fruit, and your fruit should remain" (Jn 15:16).

The Third Glorious Mystery
The Holy Spirit Descends on Mary and the Apostles

Contingent on the divine will — for God knows what is best for us — Jesus says: "Whatsoever you ask when you pray, believe that you shall receive, and [it] shall come to you" (Mk 11:24; see also Mt 21:22).

❧∾◦∾❧

The Holy Spirit knows our needs, and enters into our prayer. Paul writes: "The Spirit also helps our infirmity, for we know not what we should pray for as we ought. But the Spirit himself asks for us with unspeakable [pleading]" (Rom 8:26).

❧∾◦∾❧

Jesus' promise of sending the Holy Spirit to his apostles includes us: "But when the Paraclete shall come, whom I will send you from the Father — the Spirit of truth, who proceeds from the Father — he

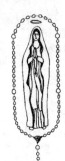

shall give testimony of me. And you shall give testimony, because you are with me from the beginning" (Jn 15:26-27).

The Fourth Glorious Mystery
Our Blessed Mother Is Assumed into Heaven

"It was inappropriate that Mary's body, which was filled with God, should crumble away into dust like our common flesh. . . . She would lie in death, as in a momentary slumber, and the passing of this Mother of Life would be as an awakening from sleep" (St. Germanus of Constantinople, +732).

❧∽ᕽᐤ∽❧

Our Blessed Mother would approve of Peter's advice: "And you, giving all diligence, join with your faith virtue . . . knowledge . . . abstinence . . . patience . . . piety . . . and brotherly love" (2 Pt 1:5-7).

❧∽ᕽᐤ∽❧

Peter tells us to avoid the impure life: "Those who walk after the flesh in the lust of uncleanness . . . shall perish in their corruption. . . . Forsaking the right way, they have gone astray, . . . They are fountains without water, and clouds tossed with whirlwinds, to whom the mist of darkness is reserved" (2 Pt 2:10-12, 15, 17).

The Fifth Glorious Mystery
Mary Is Crowned Queen of Heaven

"True devotion to Our Lady is interior, tender, holy, constant, and disinterested . . . flowing from the esteem we have for her, and our love for her" (St. Louis-Marie Grignion de Montfort, +1716).

❧◦~❦~◦❧

"[True devotion is] tender in that it is full of confidence in [the Blessed Mother], like a child's confidence in its loving mother. . . . A child implores the aid of its good Mother at all times, in all places, and about all things" (St. Louis-Marie Grignion de Montfort, +1716).

❧◦~❦~◦❧

"[True devotion is] disinterested in that it inspires the soul not to seek itself but God only, and God in his holy Mother. . . . A true client of Mary does not serve her for

selfish reasons, but because she de-
serves to be served and is so worthy of our love!" (St. Louis-Marie
Grignion de Montfort, +1716).

DAY 16

The First Joyful Mystery
The Angel Gabriel Announces to Mary That She Is to Be the Mother of God

"And the Lord God said to the serpent . . . 'I will put enmities between thee and the woman, and thy seed and her seed. She shall crush thy head, and thou shalt lie in wait for her heel' " (Gen 3:14-15).

❦

John's vision of Satan: "And there appeared . . . a great red dragon, having seven heads and ten horns. . . . His tail drew a third part of the stars of heaven, and cast them to the earth" (Apoc [Rev] 12:3-4). O Mary, protect us from the snares of the devil!

❦

Satan is vanquished: "And there was a great battle in heaven — Michael and his angels fought with the dragon, . . . And that great dragon was cast out, the old

serpent, who is called the devil, and [called] Satan, who seduces the whole world" (Apoc [Rev] 12:7, 9). My guardian angel will assist me in rejecting Satan.

The Second Joyful Mystery
Mary Visits Her Cousin Elizabeth

The evangelist tells us about John the Baptist: "And it came to pass that on the eighth day they came to circumcise the child, and they called him by his father's name, Zachary. And his mother said, 'Not so, he shall be called John' " (Lk 1:59-60).

❧⁓❦⁓❧

John would later tell his listeners: "I have baptized you with water, but he shall baptize you with the Holy Spirit" (Mk 1:8).

❧⁓❦⁓❧

Our Savior praised John the Baptist: "What went you out to see? A prophet? Yes, I tell you, and more than a prophet. For this is he of whom it is written, 'Behold, I send my [messenger] be-

fore thy face, who shall prepare thy way
before thee' " (Mt 11:9-10).

The Third Joyful Mystery
Jesus Is Born in Bethlehem

"And it came to pass, that after the
angels departed from them into heaven,
the shepherds said one to another, 'Let
us go over to Bethlehem, and let us see
this word that is come to pass, which the
Lord has shown to us' " (Lk 2:15).

✤◦✾◦✤

Paul praises those who have believed
the word of God: "Therefore, we also give
thanks to God without ceasing, because
when you had received from us the word
. . . of God, you received it not as the word
of men, but (as it truly is) the word of God,
who works in you, who have believed" (1
Thess 2:13).

✤◦✾◦✤

The "word that is come to pass" in
the angel's message is the Eternal Word,
Christ himself. John writes: "And
the Word was made flesh, and
dwelt among us" (Jn 1:14).

The Fourth Joyful Mystery
The Presentation of Jesus

Mary and Joseph followed the Mosaic Law in presenting the infant Jesus to the Father, and always sought the Father's will. Our Savior says to us: "Seek ... first the kingdom of God, and his justice, and all ... things shall be added to you" (Mt 6:33; see also Lk 12:31).

❧～❦～❧

Jesus also said: "Ask, and it shall be given; seek, and you shall find; knock, and it shall be opened to you" (Mt 7:7, Lk 11:9). Let us seek heaven's treasures!

❧～❦～❧

"If you ... know how to give good gifts to your children, how much more will your Father, who is in heaven, give good things to those who ask him?" (Mt 7:11; see also Lk 11:13).

The Fifth Joyful Mystery
Jesus Is Found in the Temple

"And he went down with them, and came to Nazareth, and was subject to them. And his mother kept all these words in her heart" (Lk 2:51).

❧◦⁓ဇ⁓◦❧

Jesus, God the Son Incarnate, gives us an example in humility, in subjecting himself to Mary and Joseph. He says to us: "Amen I say unto you — unless you be converted, and become as little children, you shall not enter the kingdom of heaven. Whosoever shall humble himself as this little child, he is the greatest in the kingdom of heaven" (Mt 18:3-4).

❧◦⁓ဇ⁓◦❧

On another occasion, Jesus said: "I give thanks to thee, O Father, Lord of heaven and earth, that thou hast hid these things from the wise and prudent, and hast revealed them to little ones" (Mt 11:25, Lk 10:21).

DAY 17

The First Sorrowful Mystery
Our Lord's Agony in the Garden

"And he [came] to his disciples, and [found] them asleep, and he [said] to Peter, 'What? Could you not watch one hour with me? Watch ... and pray, that you enter not into temptation. The spirit indeed is willing, but the flesh is weak' " (Mt 26:40-41; see also Mk 14:37-38, Lk 22:46).

❦∽❦∽❦

The sources of temptation are many. Jesus said: "Take heed and beware of all covetousness. For a man's life does not consist in the abundance of things which he possesses" (Lk 12:15).

❦∽❦∽❦

Paul warns us: "Know you not that the unjust shall not possess the kingdom of God? Be not deceived — neither fornicators, nor idolaters, nor adulterers ... nor sodomites, nor thieves, nor the covetous, nor

drunkards ... shall possess the kingdom of God" (1 Cor 6:9-10).

The Second Sorrowful Mystery
Our Lord Is Scourged

Jesus speaks to his followers: "Beware of men. For they will deliver you up in councils, and they will scourge you in their synagogues" (Mt 10:17; see also Mk 13:9, Lk 21:12).

❧～✿～❧

"And you shall be brought before governors, and before kings, for my sake, for a testimony unto them" (Mt 10:18; see also Mk 13:9, Lk 21:12-13).

❧～✿～❧

"But when they shall deliver you up, [be not anxious] how or what to speak, for it shall be given you in that hour what to speak" (Mt 10:19; see also Mk 13:11).

The Third Sorrowful Mystery

Jesus Is Crowned with Thorns

As Christ's followers, we are to expect opposition. Jesus said: "If the world hate you, know ... that it hated me before you" (Jn 15:18).

✧∼✿∼✧

We have been chosen by Christ: "If you had been of the world, the world would love its own. But because you are not of the world — I have chosen you out of the world — therefore the world hates you" (Jn 15:19; see also 17:14).

✧∼✿∼✧

"Remember the word that I said to you — the servant is not greater than his lord. If they have persecuted me, they will also persecute you; if they have kept my word, they will keep yours also" (Jn 15:20). The Holy Spirit will give us strength and courage to witness to Christ.

The Fourth Sorrowful Mystery
Jesus Carries the Cross

Our Lord died for sinners, but he warns them, and us: "If I had not come, and spoken to them, they would not have sin; but now they have no excuse for their sin" (Jn 15:22).

❧⟨∾ℰ∾⟩❧

Jesus prayed to his Father for our protection: "I do not ask that thou . . . take them out of the world, but that thou . . . preserve them from evil. They are not of the world, as I also am not of the world" (Jn 17:15-16).

❧⟨∾ℰ∾⟩❧

Once we are forgiven, let us heed our Savior's words: "Sin no more, lest some worse thing happen to thee" (Jn 5:14; see also 8:11).

The Fifth Sorrowful Mystery
Our Lord Dies on the Cross

"And Pilate wrote [an inscription], and he put it upon the cross. And the writing was, 'Jesus of Nazareth, King of the Jews' " (Jn 19:19; see also Mt 27:37, Mk 15:26, Lk 23:38).

❦∼ᵷ∼❦

We show compassion for Mary beneath the cross:

"Holy Mother, pierce me through,
In my heart each wound renew
Of my Savior crucified!"

❦∼ᵷ∼❦

"Let me share with thee his pain,
Who for all my sins was slain,
Who for me in torments died."

— Blessed Jacopone da Todi (+1306)

DAY 18

The First Glorious Mystery
Jesus Rises from the Dead

Jesus was able to read human hearts. To some he said: "Woe to you Scribes and Pharisees, hypocrites — because you are like [whitened] sepulchres, which outwardly appear . . . beautiful, but within are full of dead men's bones, and all filthiness" (Mt 23:27). May we, with God's grace, rise from the tomb of our own sins.

❧〜❦〜❧

Jesus said of the widow's mite: "Amen, I say to you, this poor widow has cast in more . . . into the treasury [than they who] cast of their abundance; but she, of her want, cast in all she had" (Mk 12:43; see also Lk 21:2-4). Let us rise above our selfishness to give of our substance to those in need.

❧〜❦〜❧

To those admiring the beauty of Jerusalem's temple,

Our Lord prophesied: "The days will come, in which there shall not be left a stone upon a stone that shall not be thrown down" (Lk 21:6). Material accomplishments, though of value, are but transitory. May we strive toward spiritual achievements, for these endure forever.

The Second Glorious Mystery
Jesus Ascends Triumphantly into Heaven

Jesus ascends to the Father, of whom he spoke: "No one knows the Son, but the Father; neither does anyone know the Father, but the Son, and he to whom the Son will reveal him" (Mt 11:27; see also Lk 10:22). May we be among those chosen to know the Father.

❧～⚜～❧

To his disciples, Jesus said of himself: "Blessed are the eyes that see the things which you see. For I say to you, many prophets and kings have desired to see the things that you see, and have not seen them — and to hear the things that you hear, and have not heard them" (Lk 10:23-24; see also Mt 13:16-17).

※〜🍂〜※

"Then was brought to [Jesus] one possessed with a devil, blind and dumb — and [Jesus] healed him, so that he both spoke and saw" (Mt 12:22). May our Divine Savior free us from Satan's bindings, to enable our eyes to see and our ears to hear Divine Revelation.

The Third Glorious Mystery
The Holy Spirit Descends on Mary and the Apostles

Recall the story of Zacchaeus. Luke writes: "He sought to see Jesus . . . and he could not for the crowd, because he was little of stature" (Lk 19:3). O Holy Spirit, increase our spiritual stature; and help us transcend material possessions, in order to see Jesus, the highest love worth having.

※〜🍂〜※

"And when Jesus came to the [tree], he looked up, and saw him, and said to him, 'Zacchaeus, make haste, and come down, for

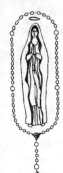

today I must abide in thy house.' And he . . . came down, and received [Jesus] with joy" (Lk 19:5-6). Honored though Zacchaeus was, we are further privileged, in frequently receiving and joyfully welcoming the Eucharistic Lord into our souls!

❧⟡❧

Of his visit to Zacchaeus, Jesus said: "For the Son of man has come to seek, and to save that which was lost" (Lk 19:10). Divine love is offered to all, but we must open our hearts.

The Fourth Glorious Mystery
Our Blessed Mother Is Assumed into Heaven

"Your stainless body did not remain within the earth. Your Son, though he is Life itself, did not exempt himself, or you, from death — but as Mother of the living God, you were worthily taken up to him" (St. John Damascene, Father and Doctor of the Church, +749).

Peter describes the Last Day: "But the day of the Lord shall come as a thief, in which the heavens shall be dissolved with heat, and the earth, and the works that are in it, shall be burned up" (2 Pt 3:10). Thus all things shall pass.

❧～§～❧

For us the Last Day will be the day of our death. Peter writes: "Wherefore, dearly beloved, waiting for these things, be diligent, that you may be found before him unspotted and blameless in peace" (2 Pt 3:14).

The Fifth Glorious Mystery
Mary Is Crowned Queen of Heaven

Mary would have us heed John's words: "My little children, let us not love in word, nor in tongue, but in deed, and in truth. . . . This is [God's] commandment — that we should believe in the name of his Son, Jesus Christ, and love one another" (1 Jn 3:18, 23).

❧～§～❧

In heaven we shall enjoy the peace and love of Christ. From his vision, John writes: "For the

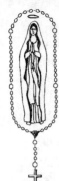

Lamb, who is in the midst of the throne, shall rule them, and shall lead them to the fountains of the waters of life, . . . And God shall wipe away all tears from their eyes — and death shall be no more, nor mourning, nor crying, nor sorrow . . . for the former things have passed away" (Apoc [Rev] 7:17, 21:4).

❦❦❦

"And I heard a voice from heaven, saying to me, 'Write — Blessed are the dead, who die in the Lord. From henceforth . . . says the Spirit, . . . they rest from their labors, for their works follow them' " (Apoc [Rev] 14:13).

DAY 19

The First Joyful Mystery

The Angel Gabriel Announces to Mary That She Is to Be the Mother of God

"*Hail, full of grace* (Lk 1:28). By these words the angel shows that Mary was altogether excluded from the wrath of the first sentence, and restored to the full grace of blessing" (St. Augustine, Father and Doctor of the Church, +430).

❧∼᪥∼❧

"The Archangel Gabriel saluted Mary as blessed among women (Lk 1:28). Whatever of malediction was infused into our nature by Eve, was taken away by the blessing of Mary, because of the majesty of the Person who was to take flesh in her" (St. Bonaventure, Doctor of the Church, +1274).

❧∼᪥∼❧

"God resists the proud, and gives grace to the humble" (Jas 4:6).

115

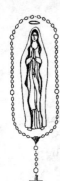

The Second Joyful Mystery
Mary Visits Her Cousin Elizabeth

"Glorious indeed, and admirable is your name, O Mary — those who pronounce it at death need not fear all the powers of hell" (St. Bonaventure, Doctor of the Church, +1274).

❦

John, Elizabeth's son and the precursor of Christ, would later acclaim his Savior: "Behold the Lamb of God; behold him who takes away the sin of the world" (Jn 1:29).

❦

In our relationship with Christ, we should follow the Baptist, who said: "He must increase, but I must decrease" (Jn 3:30).

The Third Joyful Mystery
Jesus Is Born in Bethlehem

"And the shepherds returned, glorifying and praising God, for all the things they had heard and seen, as it was told to them" (Lk 2:20).

Jesus had a special love for shepherds. Of himself he declared: "I am the good shepherd. The good shepherd gives his life for his sheep" (Jn 10:11).

✣❧✤❧✣

We are Christ's sheep, for he said: "I am the good shepherd, and I know mine, and mine know me. . . . My sheep hear my voice, and I know them, and they follow me" (Jn 10:14, 27).

The Fourth Joyful Mystery
The Presentation of Jesus

As an infant, Jesus was presented to the Father. He would later proclaim: "The works which the Father has given me to [accomplish] . . . give testimony of me, that the Father has sent me" (Jn 5:36).

✣❧✤❧✣

Jesus declared: "As the Father has life in himself, so also he has given to the Son to have life in himself. And he has given him authority to execute judgment, because he is the Son of man" (Jn 5:26-27).

✣❧✤❧✣

117

"And they who have done good shall come forth unto the resurrection of life, but they who have done evil, unto the resurrection of judgment" (Jn 5:29).

The Fifth Joyful Mystery
Jesus Is Found in the Temple

"His mother kept all these things in her heart. And Jesus increased in wisdom, and age, and grace with God and men" (Lk 2:51-52).

❦❧

Mary's heart was the perfect ground upon which the word of God was sowed. In his parable on the sower and the seed, Jesus said: "That on the good ground are they who in a good and perfect heart, hearing the word, keep it, and bring forth fruit in patience" (Lk 8:15; see also Mt 13:23, Mk 4:20).

❦❧

The apostles implored Jesus, "Increase our faith!" (Lk 17:5). Mary's faith was perfect. May she intercede with our Divine Savior to strengthen ours.

DAY 20

The First Sorrowful Mystery
Our Lord's Agony in the Garden

"Then were gathered together the chief priests, and the elders of the people, in the palace of the high priest, who was called Caiphas. And they consulted together ... [how] they might apprehend Jesus, and put him to death" (Mt 26:3-4; see also Mk 14:1, Lk 22:2).

❧∼❦∼❧

"And [Judas] said to them, 'What will you give me [for] delivering him to you?' And they assigned him thirty pieces of silver" (Mt 26:15).

❧∼❦∼❧

"And from henceforth he sought opportunity to betray [Jesus]" (Mt 26:16). We seek similar opportunity when we entertain occasions of sin.

The Second Sorrowful Mystery
Our Lord Is Scourged

"The disciples . . . leaving him, fled. . . . Then the band, and the tribune, and the servants . . . took Jesus, and bound him" (Mt 26:56, Jn 18:12).

"And the chief priests, and all the council, sought for evidence against Jesus, that they might put him to death — but they found none" (Mk 14:55; see also Mt 26:59-60).

"So Pilate . . . willing to satisfy the people, released to them Barabbas, . . . and delivered up Jesus [to be] scourged" (Mk 15:15; see also Mt 27:26, Jn 19:1).

The Third Sorrowful Mystery
Jesus Is Crowned with Thorns

The soldiers crowned Jesus a mock king. They did not realize that he was truly a king, for he had declared, "I and the Father are one" (Jn 10:30).

Matthew wrote that "great multitudes followed [Jesus], and he healed them" (Mt 19:2). Our Divine Savior healed others of pain and affliction, but he chose not to heal his own wounds, borne for love of us.

❧

Will Christ be our king, or shall we pay homage to worldly pursuits? Jesus said, "No man can serve two masters, for either he will hate the one and love the other, or he will hold to the one, and despise the other. You cannot serve God and mammon" (Mt 6:24, Lk 16:13).

The Fourth Sorrowful Mystery
Jesus Carries the Cross

Paul speaks of Jesus' love: "In [him] we have redemption through his blood, the remission of sins, according to the riches of his grace" (Eph 1:7).

❧

We show compassion for Mary:
"Is there one who would not weep,
Whelmed in miseries so
    deep,
Christ's dear Mother to
    behold?"

❧❧❧

"Can the human heart refrain
From partaking in her pain,
In that Mother's pain untold?"
— Blessed Jacopone da Todi
(+1306)

The Fifth Sorrowful Mystery
Our Lord Dies on the Cross

"The chief priests with the scribes and [elders] said, 'He saved others, himself he cannot save. If he be the king of Israel, let him now come down from the cross, and we will believe him' " (Mt 27:41-42; see also Mk 15:31-32, Lk 23:35).

❧❧❧

"He trusted in God. Let him deliver him now if he will have him, for he said, 'I am the Son of God' " (Mt 27:43).

❧❧❧

We apply these words of the Psalmist to Jesus' enemies: "There is none who does good, . . . the poison of asps is under their lips. Their mouth is full of cursing and bitterness; their feet are swift to shed blood" (Ps 13:3).

DAY 21

The First Glorious Mystery
Jesus Rises from the Dead

Jesus died and rose for our redemption and eternal life. Listen to his words: "Hear, O Israel, the Lord thy God is one God. And thou shalt love the Lord thy God with thy whole heart, and with thy whole soul, and with thy whole mind, and with thy whole strength" (Mk 12:29-30; see also Mt 22:37, Lk 10:27, Lev 19:18, Dt 6:4-5).

❧❦❧

Jesus added that the second greatest commandment is to love others as we love ourselves (see Mt 22:39, Mk 12:31, Lk 10:27). Too, though we rightly reject sin, we are not to judge another's conscience. Concerning the woman caught in adultery, Jesus declared, "He who is without sin among you, let him . . . cast a stone" (Jn 8:7).

❧❦❧

On one occasion Martha said to Mary, "The master [Jesus]

123

is come, and calls for thee" (Jn 11:28). The Master calls me too — by name — to follow him and his bidding in my life.

The Second Glorious Mystery
Jesus Ascends Triumphantly into Heaven

A requisite for our joining Christ in heaven is the virtue of humility. Jesus declared: "Amen I say to you, whosoever does not receive the kingdom of God as a little child, shall not enter into it" (Mk 10:15; see also Mt 19:14, Lk 18:17).

❧~⟡~❧

In leaving all else for Christ, we shall be rewarded. Jesus said: "And everyone who has left house, or brethren, or sisters, or father, or mother, or children, or lands, for my name's sake, shall receive a hundredfold, and shall possess life everlasting" (Mt 19:29; see also Mk 10:29-30, Lk 18:29-30).

❧~⟡~❧

At the Last Supper, Jesus had prayed to his Father: "And now I am no more in the world ... these are in the world, and I come to thee. Holy Father, keep them in thy name, whom thou hast given me — that they may be one, as we also are [one]" (Jn 17:11).

The Third Glorious Mystery
The Holy Spirit Descends on Mary and the Apostles

The Holy Spirit is Divine Love. In divine love Jesus cured affliction. Matthew writes: "The multitudes marvelled, seeing the dumb speak, the lame walk, the blind see — and they glorified the God of Israel" (Mt 15:31; see also Mk 7:37).

❦

From the concern of divine love, Jesus cast out evil spirits: "And there was in their synagogue a man with an unclean spirit, and he cried out, 'What have we to do with thee, Jesus of Nazareth? Art thou come to destroy us? I know who thou art, the holy one of God.' [Jesus replied:] 'Speak no more, and go out of the man.' And the unclean spirit ... crying out with a loud voice, went

out of him" (Mk 1:23-26; see also Lk 4:33-35).

We are to be temples of divine love. Paul writes: "Know you not that [you] are temples of the Holy Spirit, who is in you, whom you have from God, and you are not your own? For you are bought with a great price — glorify and bear God in your body" (1 Cor 6:19-20).

The Fourth Glorious Mystery
Our Blessed Mother Is Assumed into Heaven

"*Arise, O Lord, into your resting place — thou and the Ark which thou hast sanctified* (Ps 131 [132]:8). The Lord arose when he ascended to the right hand of the Father. The ark which he has sanctified arose when the Virgin Mother was assumed to the heavenly bridal chamber" (St. Anthony of Padua, Doctor of the Church, +1231).

From the Book of Proverbs, Mary would say to us: "Have confidence in the

Lord with all thy heart, and lean not upon thine own prudence. In all thy ways think of him, and he will direct thy steps" (Prv 3:5-6).

†⸱⸱⸱⸱⸱⸱

"My [child], reject not the correction of the Lord, and do not faint when thou art chastised by him. For whom the Lord loves, he chastises" (Prv 3:11-12).

The Fifth Glorious Mystery
Mary Is Crowned Queen of Heaven

With Mary and the saints let us praise God. In his vision, John writes: "I saw a great multitude, which no man could number, of all nations, and tribes, and peoples, and tongues — standing before the throne, and in sight of the Lamb, . . . And they cried with a loud voice, saying, 'Salvation to our God, who is seated upon the throne, and to the Lamb' " (Apoc [Rev] 7:9-10).

†⸱⸱⸱⸱⸱⸱

"And all the angels . . . fell upon their faces before the throne, and adored God, saying . . . 'Benediction and glory, and

wisdom, and thanksgiving, honor, and power, and strength to our God for ever and ever' " (Apoc [Rev] 7:11-12).

❧∼❦∼❧

In John's vision, God speaks: "And he who sat on the throne said, 'Behold, I make all things new. . . . I am Alpha and Omega, the beginning and the end. To him who thirsts I will give the fountain of the water of life' " (Apoc [Rev] 21:5-6).

DAY 22

The First Joyful Mystery

The Angel Gabriel Announces to Mary That She Is to Be the Mother of God

The Father declared Jesus to be his beloved Son (see Mt 3:17, 17:5; Mk 1:11, 9:6; Lk 3:22, 9:35). The Father enabled Mary to become the mother of his Incarnate Son.

❧∽❦∽❧

Jesus said that no one "can serve two masters" (see Mt 6:24, Lk 16:13). Our Blessed Lady served God with her whole heart, her whole mind, and her whole soul. Let us imitate her allegiance!

❧∽❦∽❧

Jesus tells us: "A good tree cannot yield bad fruit; neither can a bad tree yield good fruit. . . . By their fruits you shall know them" (Mt 7:18, 20). Mary was the tree that bore the fruit of eternal life, our Divine Savior. May we bring forth fruit pleasing to God.

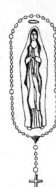

The Second Joyful Mystery
Mary Visits Her Cousin Elizabeth

"And Zachary was filled with the Holy Spirit, and he prophesied, saying, 'Blessed be the Lord God of Israel, because he has visited and wrought the redemption of his people' " (Lk 1:67-68).

✣∿✿∿✣

Jesus warns us: "The time is [fulfilled], and the kingdom of God is at hand. Repent, and believe the gospel" (Mk 1:15; see also Mt 4:17).

✣∿✿∿✣

Paul writes: "Christ died for us. Much more, therefore, being now justified by his blood, shall we be saved from wrath through him" (Rom 5:9).

The Third Joyful Mystery
Jesus Is Born in Bethlehem

"Now when Jesus was born in Bethlehem of Judea, in the days of King Herod, behold, there came wise men from the east to Jerusalem, saying, 'Where is he who is born king of the Jews? For we have seen his star in the east, and [have] come to adore him'" (Mt 2:1-2).

❧⤚⟡⤙❧

"A star shall rise out of Jacob, and a sceptre shall spring up from Israel" (Num 24:17).

❧⤚⟡⤙❧

"He shone in his days as the morning star in the midst of a cloud, and as the moon at the full" (Eccles [Sir] 50:6). May we reflect the light of Jesus to all whom we encounter!

The Fourth Joyful Mystery
The Presentation of Jesus

"And after they had performed all things according to the law of the Lord, they returned into Galilee, to their own city, Nazareth. And the child grew, and waxed strong, full of wisdom, and the grace of God was in him" (Lk 2:39-40).

⁂

Mary offered Jesus to his Father. Paul writes: "Walk in love, as Christ also has loved us, and has delivered himself for us, an oblation and a sacrifice to God, for [a fragrance] of sweetness" (Eph 5:2).

⁂

In his letter to the Hebrews, Paul cites Psalm 39:7, with reference to Christ: "Sacrifice and oblation thou wouldst not. . . . Then said I, 'Behold I come . . . that I should do thy will, O God' " (Heb 10:5, 7).

The Fifth Joyful Mystery
Jesus Is Found in the Temple

Jesus enthralled his hearers in the Temple, but his wisdom and teaching were not always favorably received. Later he would declare: "The men of Ninive shall rise in judgment with this generation, and shall condemn it — because they did penance at the preaching of Jonah. And behold, a greater than Jonah is here" (Mt 12:41; see also Lk 11:32).

❦

To those who follow him, Our Lord promised: "I give them life everlasting, and they shall not perish forever, and no man can snatch them out of my hand" (Jn 10:28).

❦

To be Jesus' disciple is to carry one's cross: "He who takes not up his cross and follows me is not worthy of me. He who finds his life shall lose it, and he who [loses] his life for my sake shall find it" (Mt 10:38-39).

DAY 23

The First Sorrowful Mystery
Our Lord's Agony in the Garden

At the Last Supper, with reference to his betrayer, Jesus had cited the Scriptures: "He who eats bread with me, shall lift up his heel against me" (Jn 13:18; see also Ps 40:10). We join in Judas's betrayal by our own sins.

❧❦❧

Peter was later to say of Judas: "He indeed has possessed a field of the reward of iniquity, and being hanged, burst asunder . . . and all his bowels gushed out" (Acts 1:18). Judas succumbed to Satan, whom Jesus called a murderer and the father of lies (see Jn 8:44).

❧❦❧

Peter continues: "For it is written in the book of Psalms — Let their habitation become desolate, and let there be none to dwell therein, and let another take his [office]" (Acts 1:20).

And so it will be with us, if we fail our Christian calling.

The Second Sorrowful Mystery
Our Lord Is Scourged

Our Divine Savior is treated with sacrilege in the presence of the high priests: "One of the [attendants] standing by gave Jesus a blow, saying, 'Answer thou the high priest so?' Jesus answered him, 'If I have spoken ill, give testimony . . . but if well, why [strike] me?' " (Jn 18:22-23).

❧◦❦◦❧

"Then they spit in his face, and buffeted him, and others struck his face with the palms of their hands, saying, 'Prophesy unto us, O Christ — who is [it] that struck thee?' " (Mt 26:67-68; see also Mk 14:65, Lk 22:63-64).

❧◦❦◦❧

As Jeremiah the prophet had spoken: "He shall give his cheek to him who strikes him — he shall be filled with reproaches" (Lam 3:30).

The Third Sorrowful Mystery
Jesus Is Crowned with Thorns

When enduring hardship with and for Christ, let us remember Paul's words: "We suffer tribulation, but are not distressed; we are straitened, but are not destitute" (2 Cor 4:8).

❧∽ᵹ∽❧

"We suffer persecution, but are not forsaken; we are cast down, but we perish not" (2 Cor 4:9).

❧∽ᵹ∽❧

"Always bearing . . . in our body the dying of Jesus, that the life also of Jesus may be made manifest in our bodies" (2 Cor 4:10).

The Fourth Sorrowful Mystery
Jesus Carries the Cross

The evangelist writes: "And it was the third hour, and they crucified him" (Mk 15:25).

❧～✿～❧

Let us say to Mary:
"Let me mingle tears with thee,
Mourning him who mourned for
　me,
All the days that I may live . . ."

❧～✿～❧

"By the Cross with thee to stay,
There with thee to weep and pray,
Is all I ask of thee to give."
— Blessed Jacopone da Todi (+1306)

The Fifth Sorrowful Mystery
Our Lord Dies on the Cross

As we stand beneath the cross, we should be mindful of the hour of our own death. Jesus exhorts us: "Watch you, therefore, because you know not when the lord of the house comes. . . . Watch you, therefore, because you know not the day nor the hour" (Mk 13:35, Mt 25:13).

❧～⋆～❧

We show compassion for his Mother:
"At the Cross her station keeping,
Stood the mournful Mother
    weeping,
Close to Jesus to the last . . ."

❧～⋆～❧

"Through her heart his sorrow
    sharing,
All his bitter anguish bearing,
Now at length the sword has
    passed."
— Blessed Jacopone da Todi (+1306)

DAY 24

The First Glorious Mystery
Jesus Rises from the Dead

Death as we know it was not God's will for humanity, but rather the consequence of original sin. Jesus, fully human as well as divine, shared our grief of bereavement, for example, upon the death of Joseph. And the sorrow he felt over the death of his friend Lazarus is expressed touchingly by John, who writes simply: "And Jesus wept" (Jn 11:35).

❧∼ॐ∼❧

At that occasion, Jesus showed his divine power over death. John writes: "He cried out with a loud voice, 'Lazarus, come forth!' . . . He that had been dead came forth, bound feet and hands. . . . Jesus said to [those present], 'Loose him, and let him go'" (Jn 11:43-44).

❧∼ॐ∼❧

We were bound in the death of sin. But our Divine Savior has loosed our bonds, and bids us to

141

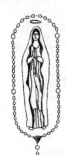

come forth to a new beginning —
and a new life — in him (see Jn
11:44-45).

The Second Glorious Mystery
Jesus Ascends Triumphantly into Heaven

This is the story of Emmaus:
"And it came to pass, while he was
at table with them, he took bread,
and blessed, and broke, and gave
to them. And their eyes were opened, and
they knew him — and he vanished out of
their sight" (Lk 24:30-31).

❧～❦～❧

Luke pointedly writes of the early
Christians: "They were persevering in the
doctrine of the apostles, and in . . . the
breaking of the bread, and in prayers"
(Acts 2:42).

❧～❦～❧

We are privileged to receive Divine
Bread in the Eucharistic liturgy. Paul
writes: "For I have received of the Lord
that which also I delivered to you, that
the Lord Jesus, [on] the night in which
he was betrayed, took bread, and giving

thanks, broke, and said, 'Take you, and eat — this is my body, which shall be delivered for you. Do this for the commemoration of me' " (1 Cor 11:23-24).

The Third Glorious Mystery
The Holy Spirit Descends on Mary and the Apostles

Jesus warns: "Therefore I say to you: Every sin and blasphemy shall be forgiven men, but the blasphemy against the Spirit shall not be forgiven. . . . He that shall speak against the Holy Spirit, it shall not be forgiven him neither in this world, nor in the world to come" (Mt 12:31-32; see also Mk 3:28-29).

&~§~&

The Holy Spirit gives unity to Christ's Church. Our Lord said: "He who is not with me, is against me, and he who gathers not with me, scatters" (Mt 12:30, Lk 11:23).

&~§~&

By heeding the voice of the Magisterium, which is guided by the Holy Spirit, we shall avoid falling into heresy. Jesus, who es-

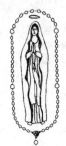

tablished the apostolic succession, declared: "Amen, amen, I say to you, he who receives whomever I send, receives me, and he who receives me receives him who sent me" (Jn 13:20).

The Fourth Glorious Mystery
Our Blessed Mother Is Assumed into Heaven

Someday we shall join Mary in heaven. In the Scriptures we read: "The souls of the just are in the hand of God, and the torment of death shall not touch them. In the sight of the unwise they seemed to die . . . but they are in peace. And . . . their hope is full of immortality" (Wis 3:1-4).

✤৵ৎৡৣৎ৵✤

Our devotion to Mary is described in the Book of Wisdom: "There is great delight in her friendship, and inexhaustible riches in the works of her hands" (Wis 8:18).

✤৵ৎৡৣৎ৵✤

We apply these words from the Book of Ecclesiasticus (Sirach) to Mary's lips:

"I am the mother of fair love, and of fear, and of knowledge, and of holy hope. In me is all grace of the way and of the truth; in me is all hope of life and of virtue" (Eccles 24:24-25).

The Fifth Glorious Mystery
Mary Is Crowned Queen of Heaven

Our Blessed Mother will grant us the seventh gift of the Holy Spirit — fear of the Lord (see Is 11:3). In the Book of Ecclesiasticus (Sirach) we read: "The fear of the Lord is honor, and glory, and gladness, and a crown of joy. The fear of the Lord shall delight the heart, and shall give joy, and gladness, and length of days" (Eccles 1:11-12).

❧❧❧

"It shall go well with him who fears the Lord, and in the days of his end he shall be blessed" (Eccles 1:19).

❧❧❧

"The fear of the Lord drives out sin. . . . For the fear of the Lord is wisdom and discipline" (Eccles 1:27, 34).

DAY 25

The First Joyful Mystery

**The Angel Gabriel Announces to Mary
That She Is to Be the Mother of God**

God loved us — and planned our redemption — even before we knew him. John writes: "In this is [love]; not as if we have loved God, but because he first loved us, and sent his Son as a propitiation for our sins" (1 Jn 4:10).

❖〜✟〜❖

Divine love invites a response. God said to Moses: "I am the Lord thy God . . . showing mercy to thousands . . . to those who love me, and keep my commandments" (Ex 20:5, 6).

❖〜✟〜❖

In the Book of Deuteronomy we read: "Thou shalt love the Lord thy God with thy whole heart, and with thy whole soul, and with thy whole strength" (Deut 6:5).

The Second Joyful Mystery
Mary Visits Her Cousin Elizabeth

May we follow Mary's example in fulfilling the second commandment, "Thou shalt love thy neighbor as thyself" (Mt 19:19; see also Mk 12:31, Lk 10:27, Rom 13:9, Gal 5:14, Jas 2:8).

❧⁓ᵹ⁓❧

In the Book of Ecclesiasticus (Sirach) we read: "Remember not any injury done thee by thy neighbor, and do thou nothing by deeds of injury. . . . Forgive thy neighbor if he has hurt thee — then shall thy sins be forgiven . . . when thou prayest" (Eccles 10:6, 28:2).

❧⁓ᵹ⁓❧

We also read: "Remember the fear of God, and be not angry with thy neighbor" (Eccles 28:8). Let us ask our Blessed Mother to obtain for us the grace to be at peace with all.

The Third Joyful Mystery
Jesus Is Born in Bethlehem

The Wise Men offered gifts (see Mt 2:11). The gold symbolized Jesus' kingship, the frankincense his divinity and priesthood, and the myrrh his humanity and his death for our sins.

※～ॐ～※

Jesus speaks to us: "If thou offer thy gift at the altar, and there remember that thy brother has anything against thee, leave thy gift before the altar. First go to be reconciled to thy brother, and then come and offer thy gift" (Mt 5:23-24).

※～ॐ～※

In the Lord's Prayer, Jesus taught us to forgive others' offenses (see Mt 6:12-15, Lk 11:4). Through grace such an act of love becomes possible.

The Fourth Joyful Mystery
The Presentation of Jesus

Mary and Joseph fulfilled the Mosaic Law. In Exodus we read: "And the Lord spoke to Moses, saying, 'Sanctify unto me every first-born that opens the womb among the children of Israel'" (Ex 13:1-2).

❧～✽～❧

We apply these words from the Book of Ecclesiasticus (Sirach) to Mary: "And so was I established in Sion, and in the holy city likewise I rested, and my power was in Jerusalem" (Eccles 24:15).

❧～✽～❧

As Jesus is presented to his Father, we praise God with the song of the Seraphim: "Holy, holy, holy, the Lord God of hosts! All the earth is full of his glory!" (Is 6:3).

The Fifth Joyful Mystery
Jesus Is Found in the Temple

We should constantly seek the Lord: "And when thou shalt seek the Lord, thou shalt find him . . . if thou seek him with all thy heart, and all the affliction of thy soul" (Deut 4:29).

※～ᡝ～※

In the Psalms we read: "The poor shall eat and shall be filled. And they shall praise the Lord — [those] who seek him. Their hearts shall live for ever and ever" (Ps 21:27).

※～ᡝ～※

Let us pray with David: "My face has sought thee; thy face, O Lord, I will seek. . . . Be thou my helper, forsake me not. Do not thou despise me, O God my Savior" (Ps 26:8-9).

DAY 26

The First Sorrowful Mystery
Our Lord's Agony in the Garden

"Satan entered into Judas, who was surnamed Iscariot, one of the twelve. And he went, and discoursed with the chief priests, and the magistrates, how he might betray [Jesus] to them" (Lk 22:3-4).

❧❦❧

At the Last Supper Jesus said: "He who dips his hand with me in the dish, the same shall betray me. . . . But woe to that man, by whom the Son of man shall be betrayed. It were better for that man if he had not been born" (Mt 26:23-24; see also Mk 14:20-21, Lk 22:21-22, Jn 13:25-26). Whether or not Judas was reconciled to God at the moment of death is unknown. But Jesus' point is clear: It would be better not to have been born than to die in unrepented mortal sin!

❧❦❧

Paul encourages us: "Brethren, be strengthened in the Lord,

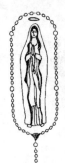

and in the might of his power. Put you on the armor of God, that you may be able to stand against the snares of the devil" (Eph 6:10-11).

The Second Sorrowful Mystery
Our Lord Is Scourged

Mark writes that Jesus always had compassion on the crowds that followed him, because "they were like sheep without a shepherd" (Mk 6:34). The Shepherd has now become a sacrificial Lamb — led to slaughter because of our sins.

✢✣✤✣✢

Peter had earlier attempted to prevent Jesus' arrest. But our Savior said to him, "Put up thy sword into the scabbard. The chalice which my Father has given me — shall I not drink it?" (Jn 18:11).

✢✣✤✣✢

Paul speaks: "[God] spared not even his own Son, but delivered him up for us all — has he not also, with him, given us all things?" (Rom 8:32).

The Third Sorrowful Mystery
Jesus Is Crowned with Thorns

Paul tells us: "For there is one God, and one mediator of God and men, the man Jesus Christ — who gave himself [as] a redemption for all" (1 Tm 2:5-6).

❧~❦~❧

Let us ask of Mary:
"Virgin of all virgins blest,
Listen to my fond request,
Let me share thy grief divine."

❧~❦~❧

"Let me to my latest breath,
In my body bear the death
of that dying Son of thine."
— Blessed Jacopone da Todi (+1306)

155

The Fourth Sorrowful Mystery
Jesus Carries the Cross

Peter urges us: "Suffer patiently — this is thankworthy before God. For unto this you have been called, because Christ suffered also for us, leaving you an example that you should follow in his steps" (1 Pt 2:20-21).

❦

Let us therefore unite our suffering with Christ's. Paul writes: "We are the [children] of God, and if [children], heirs also — heirs indeed of God, and joint-heirs with Christ. . . . If we suffer with him, we [shall] be also glorified with him" (Rom 8:16-17).

❦

Paul continues: "For I reckon that the sufferings of this present time are not worthy to be compared with the glory to come" (Rom 8:18).

The Fifth Sorrowful Mystery
Our Lord Dies on the Cross

The evangelist writes: "And there were many women [standing at a distance], who had followed Jesus from Galilee, ministering to him. Among whom was Mary Magdalene, and Mary the mother of James and Joseph, and the mother of the sons of Zebedee" (Mt 27:55-56; see also Mk 15:40; Lk 23:49).

❧❦❧

Our Savior speaks to us: "This is my commandment — that you love one another as I have loved you" (Jn 15:12).

❧❦❧

"Greater love than this no man has, that a man lay down his life for his friends" (Jn 15:13).

DAY 27

The First Glorious Mystery
Jesus Rises from the Dead

With reference to our life on earth, Paul writes: "For whether we live, we live to the Lord. Or whether we die, we die to the Lord. Therefore, whether we live or whether we die, we are the Lord's" (Rom 14:8).

✤⟋⟋⟍✤

We were created for immortal life. Jesus said: "Have you not read that which was spoken by God, saying . . . 'I am the God of Abraham, and the God of Isaac, and the God of Jacob'? He is not the God of the dead, but of the living" (Mt 22:31-32; see also Mk 12:26-27, Lk 20:37-38).

✤⟋⟋⟍✤

We live eternally in Christ. Paul writes: "Christ is risen from the dead, the firstfruits of those who sleep. . . . And as in Adam all die, so also in Christ all shall be made alive" (1 Cor 15:20, 22).

The Second Glorious Mystery
Jesus Ascends Triumphantly into Heaven

To enter heaven, we must have the garment of grace at the moment of death. In Jesus' parable of the marriage feast, we read: "And the king went in to see the wedding guests, and he saw there a man who had not on a wedding garment. . . . Then the king said to the waiters, '. . . cast him into the exterior darkness, [where] there shall be weeping and gnashing of teeth' " (Mt 22:11, 13).

※～❦～※

We should live continually in the state of grace. Paul writes: "Now being free from sin, and [having] become servants of God, you have your [reward] unto sanctification, and the end [of] everlasting life. For the wages of sin is death, but the grace of God is everlasting life, in Christ Jesus, our Lord" (Rom 6:22-23).

※～❦～※

Penance is necessary in the fight against sin. Paul declares: "I so fight, not as one beating the air. But I chastise my body, and bring it into subjection" (1 Cor 9:26-27).

The Third Glorious Mystery
The Holy Spirit Descends on Mary and the Apostles

The Holy Spirit brings us to the unity prayed for by our Blessed Lord — that unity which testifies to his truth. Jesus implores the Father, saying: "That they all may be one, as thou, Father, in me, and I in thee, that they also may be one in us — that the world may believe that thou hast sent me" (Jn 17:21).

❦❧

Jesus' unity reflects the love between Father and Son: "I in them, and thou in me, that they may be made perfect in one — and that the world may know that thou hast sent me, and hast loved them, as thou hast also loved me" (Jn 17:23).

❦❧

"And I have made known thy name to them, and will make it known — that the love wherewith thou hast loved me, may be in them, and I in them" (Jn 17:26).

The Fourth Glorious Mystery
Our Blessed Mother Is Assumed into Heaven

"Mary's holy body is enjoying the bliss worthy of her through whom Light shone upon the world! In her immortal and glorified body, she received the reward of her chastity and her martyrdom" (St. Epiphanius of Salamis, +403).

✦✧❦✧✦

With words from the Book of Wisdom, we can say of Mary: "For she knows and understands all things, and shall lead me . . . in my works, and shall preserve me by her power" (Wis 9:11).

✦✧❦✧✦

We place these words from the Book of Ecclesiasticus (Sirach) upon Mary's lips: "My [child], if thou wilt attend to me, thou shalt learn. . . . If thou wilt incline thy ear, thou shalt receive instruction, and if thou love to hear, thou shalt be wise" (Eccles 6:33-34).

The Fifth Glorious Mystery
Mary Is Crowned Queen of Heaven

Scriptural passages from the Book of Proverbs describe our devotion to Mary: "She is more precious than all riches, and all the things that are desired are not to be compared with her. . . . Her ways are beautiful ways, and all her paths are peaceable" (Prv 3:15, 17).

✦⦿✦

"She is a tree of life to those [who] hold on to her, and he who [retains] her is blessed" (Prv 3:18).

✦⦿✦

"Forsake her not, and she shall keep thee; love her, and she shall preserve thee. . . . She shall give [thee] increase of graces, and protect thee with a noble crown" (Prv 4:6, 9).

DAY 28

The First Joyful Mystery

The Angel Gabriel Announces to Mary That She Is to Be the Mother of God

John speaks to us: "We have seen, and do bear witness, and declare unto you eternal life, which was with the Father, and has appeared to us" (1 Jn 1:2).

❧⚜❧

"That which we have seen and have heard, we declare unto you, that you also may have fellowship with us, and our fellowship may be with the Father, and with his Son, Jesus Christ" (1 Jn 1:3).

❧⚜❧

How fortunate are we, who have received the gift of faith. In John's letter we read: "And these things we write to you, that you may rejoice, and your joy may be full" (1 Jn 1:4).

The Second Joyful Mystery
Mary Visits Her Cousin Elizabeth

Zachary praises God: "[All this is the work] of the tender mercy of our God by which the daybreak from on high will visit us to shine on those who sit in darkness and death's shadow, to guide our feet into the path of peace" (Lk 1:78-79).

※～❦～※

John writes: "And this is the declaration which we have heard from him, and declare unto you — that God is light, and that in him there is no darkness" (1 Jn 1:5).

※～❦～※

"If we walk in the light, as he also is in the light, we have fellowship one toward another — and the blood of Jesus Christ, his Son, cleanses us from all sin" (1 Jn 1:7).

The Third Joyful Mystery
Jesus Is Born in Bethlehem

John tells us: "He was in the world, and the world was made by him, and the world knew him not. He came unto his own, and his own received him not" (Jn 1:10-11).

❧❦

The evangelist points out: "And this is the judgment — the light has come into the world, and men loved darkness rather than the light, for their works were evil" (Jn 3:19).

❧❦

Jesus speaks to us: "I, the light, am come into the world — that whosoever believes in me, may not remain in darkness" (Jn 12:46).

The Fourth Joyful Mystery
The Presentation of Jesus

Although Mary fulfilled the Law, a wise saint says: "The Virgin was not subject to the law of purification, since without human generation she became Emmanuel's mother — pure and undefiled. And, having become a mother, she remained still a virgin" (St. Basil the Great, Doctor of the Church, +379).

❧❧❧

"Hail, full of grace! You are the golden urn containing Manna from heaven!" (St. Epiphanius of Salamis, +403).

❧❧❧

"Praise me also for the spotless and perfect virginity of her who conceived me as a virgin, bore me as a virgin, and virgin remained after childbirth — ever imitating my innocence" (words of Jesus to St. Gertrude the Great, +1302).

The Fifth Joyful Mystery
Jesus Is Found in the Temple

Jesus was found in the Temple of Jerusalem (see Lk 2:46). We can find him in the living tabernacle of God — the Immaculate Heart of Mary.

※∿҉∿※

In the Book of Canticle of Canticles (Song of Songs), we read: "Thy neck is as the tower of David . . . a thousand bucklers hang upon it, all the armor of valiant men" (Cant 4:4). This passage has been applied to Mary, for she is that tower against which Satan cannot prevail.

※∿҉∿※

Solomon adorned the Temple of Jerusalem with the finest gold (see 3 Kgs [1 Kgs] 6:20-22). Mary, the Temple of the Holy Spirit, was fully adorned with his priceless sevenfold gifts.

The First Sorrowful Mystery
Our Lord's Agony in the Garden

"Then Judas, who betrayed him, seeing that he was condemned, repenting himself, brought back the thirty pieces of silver to the chief priests and the [elders], saying, 'I have betrayed innocent blood'" (Mt 27:3-4).

❧～✿～❧

"And casting down the pieces of silver in the temple, he departed, and went and hanged himself with a halter" (Mt 27:5). May we never despair of God's mercy!

❧～✿～❧

Paul cautions us: "For our wrestling is not against flesh and blood, but against principalities and powers, against the rulers of this darkness, against the spirits of wickedness" (Eph 6:12).

The Second Sorrowful Mystery
Our Lord Is Scourged

Paul asks: "How much more shall the blood of Christ, who, through the Holy Spirit, offered himself without spot to God, cleanse our conscience from dead works, to serve the living God?" (Heb 9:14).

❧∾⸎∽❧

In the Book of Revelation (Apocalypse) John writes: "And he was clothed with a garment sprinkled with blood, and his name is called, the Word of God" (Apoc 19:13).

❧∾⸎∽❧

If we love Christ, we shall follow Paul's admonition: "Dearly beloved, let us cleanse ourselves from all defilement of the flesh and of the spirit, perfecting sanctification in the fear of God" (2 Cor 7:1).

The Third Sorrowful Mystery
Jesus Is Crowned with Thorns

John speaks: "In this we have known the [love] of God, because he has laid down his life for us — and we ought to lay down our lives for the brethren" (1 Jn 3:16).

We ask of Mary:

"Wounded with his every wound,
Steep my soul till it hath swooned
In his very blood away."

✥⟶ᕯ⟵✥

"Be to me, O Virgin, nigh,
Lest in flames I burn and die,
In that awful Judgment Day."
— Blessed Jacopone da Todi (+1306)

The Fourth Sorrowful Mystery
Jesus Carries the Cross

Paul speaks: "Who then shall separate us from Christ? Shall tribulation? Or distress? Or famine? Or nakedness? Or danger? Or persecution? Or the sword? . . . But in all these things we overcome, because of him who has loved us" (Rom 8:35, 37).

✥⟶ᕯ⟵✥

Paul urges us: "In all things let us exhibit ourselves as the ministers of God, in much patience, in tribulation, in necessities, in distresses, in stripes, in prisons . . . in labors

173

. . . in fastings . . . in long suffering"
(2 Cor 6:4-6).

❧～ℰ～❧

"As dying, and behold we live;
as chastised, and not killed; as sorrowful, yet always rejoicing; . . . as
having nothing, and possessing all
things" (2 Cor 6:9-10).

The Fifth Sorrowful Mystery
Our Lord Dies on the Cross

"Jesus . . . having loved his
own . . . loved them to the end" (Jn 13:1).

❧～ℰ～❧

We beseech our Divine Savior:
"Christ, when thou shalt call me
　　hence,
Be thy Mother my defense,
Be thy Cross my victory."

❧～ℰ～❧

"While my body here decays,
May my soul thy goodness praise,
Safe in Paradise with thee!"
— Blessed Jacopone da Todi (+1306)

DAY 30

The First Glorious Mystery
Jesus Rises from the Dead

Redeemed by Christ, we should re-form our lives. Paul writes: "For they who are according to the flesh, relish the things that are of the flesh — but those who are according to the spirit, mind the things that are of the spirit. For the wisdom of the flesh is death, but the wisdom of the spirit is life and peace" (Rom 8:5-6).

❦

"Whosoever are led by the Spirit of God, they are the [children] of God. For you have not received the spirit of bond-age again in fear — but you have received the spirit of adoption of [children], whereby we cry, 'Abba' ('Father')" (Rom 8:14-15).

❦

According to Paul, God protects and takes care of us: "We know that to those who love God, all things work together unto good — to

[those] called to be saints" (Rom 8:28).

The Second Glorious Mystery
Jesus Ascends Triumphantly into Heaven

Jesus will come again, for he declared: "The Son of man shall send his angels, and they shall gather out of his kingdom . . . those who work iniquity, and shall cast them into the furnace of fire, [where] there shall be weeping and gnashing of teeth. Then shall the just shine as the sun, in the kingdom of their Father. He who has ears to hear, let him hear" (Mt 13:41-43).

❧⟡❧

Paul instructs us: "Purge out the old leaven, that you may be new. . . . Christ, our Pasch, is sacrificed — therefore let us feast, not with . . . the leaven of malice and wickedness, but with the unleavened bread of sincerity and truth" (1 Cor 5:7-8).

❧⟡❧

The apostle encourages us: "God is faithful, [and] will not suffer you to be tempted above that which you are able, [but will enable you] to bear it" (1 Cor 10:13).

The Third Glorious Mystery
The Holy Spirit Descends on Mary and the Apostles

Mary, the immaculate spouse of the Holy Spirit, was with the disciples as they awaited the coming of the Spirit. Luke writes: "All these were persevering with one mind in prayer with the women, and Mary, the mother of Jesus, and his brethren" (Acts 1:14).

✣∾❦∾✣

The early Christians were vivified by the Holy Spirit. We read: "And when they prayed, the place was shaken wherein they were assembled. And they were all filled with the Holy Spirit, and they spoke the word of God with confidence" (Acts 4:31).

✣∾❦∾✣

The early Church lived in harmonious community: "And all who believed were together, and had all things [in] common. . . . And the multitude of believers had but

one heart and one soul" (Acts 2:44, 4:32).

The Fourth Glorious Mystery
Our Blessed Mother Is Assumed into Heaven

Mary is the spiritual rainbow uniting us on earth with her Divine Son in heaven. In the Book of Ecclesiasticus (Sirach) we read: "Look upon the rainbow, and bless him who made it. It is very beautiful in its brightness. It encompasses the heaven about with the circle of its glory, the hands of the Most High have displayed it" (Eccles 43:12-13).

Other passages in the Book of Ecclesiasticus (Sirach) symbolize Our Blessed Lady: "As the rainbow giving light in the bright clouds, and as the flower of roses . . . that are on the brink of the water, and as the sweet smelling frankincense" (Eccles 50:8).

"O Mary, you are the ark of Noah and the rainbow. . . . You are the ladder that Jacob saw going up to heaven. . . . You are the book of Moses, whereon the New Covenant is written with the finger of God. . . . Hail, special honor of all the saints!" (St. Tarasius, Patriarch of Constantinople, +806).

The Fifth Glorious Mystery
Mary Is Crowned Queen of Heaven

Let us sing a hymn in honor of our Heavenly Queen:

"O glorious Lady! Throned on high
Above the star-illumined sky,
Thereto ordained, thy bosom lent
To thy Creator nourishment."

❦⁓ℰ⁓❦

"Through thy sweet Offspring we
    receive
The bliss once lost through
    hapless Eve,
And heaven to mortals open lies
Now thou art Portal of the
    skies."

❦⁓ℰ⁓❦

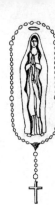

"Thou art the door of Heaven's
  high King,
Light's Gateway fair and
  glistening,
Life through a Virgin was
  restored,
Ye ransomed nations, praise the
  Lord!"

  — Ascribed to St. Venantius
Fortunatus (+609) or to St. Anthony
of Padua, Doctor of the Church
(+1231)

Prayers of the Rosary

The Apostles' Creed

I believe in God the Father Almighty, Creator of heaven and earth; and in Jesus Christ, His only Son, Our Lord; who was conceived by the Holy Spirit, born of the Virgin Mary, suffered under Pontius Pilate, was crucified, died, and was buried. He descended into hell; the third day he rose again from the dead. He ascended into heaven, and is seated at the right hand of God, the Father Almighty; from thence he shall come to judge the living and the dead. I believe in the Holy Spirit, the holy Catholic Church, the communion of saints, the forgiveness of sins, the resurrection of the body, and life everlasting. Amen.

The Our Father

Our Father, who art in heaven, hallowed be Thy Name! Thy kingdom come, Thy will be done, on earth as it is in heaven. Give us this day our daily bread; and forgive us our trespasses, as we forgive those who trespass against us; and lead us not into temptation, but deliver us from evil. Amen.

The Hail Mary

Hail Mary, full of grace, the Lord is with thee! Blessed art thou among women, and blessed is the fruit of thy womb, Jesus. Holy Mary, Mother of God, pray for us sinners now, and at the hour of our death. Amen.

The Glory Be to the Father

Glory be to the Father, and to the Son, and to the Holy Spirit! As it was in the beginning, is now, and ever shall be, world without end. Amen.

The Fátima Prayer

O my Jesus, forgive us our sins, save us from the fires of hell. Lead all souls to heaven, especially those most in need of thy mercy.

The Hail, Holy Queen

Hail, Holy Queen, Mother of Mercy, hail, our life, our sweetness, and our hope! To thee do we cry, poor banished children of Eve. To thee do we send up our sighs, mourning and weeping in this valley of tears. Turn then, most gracious Advocate, thine eyes of mercy toward us; and after this our exile, show unto us the blessed fruit of thy womb, Jesus! O clement, O loving, O sweet Virgin Mary!

Pray for us, O holy Mother of God.

That we may be made worthy of the promises of Christ.

LET US PRAY

O God, whose only-begotten Son, by His life, death, and resurrection, has purchased for us the rewards of eternal life; grant, we beseech Thee, that meditating on these mysteries of the most holy Rosary of the Blessed Virgin Mary, we may imitate what they contain and obtain what they promise. Through the same Christ, Our Lord. Amen.

Promises Made by the Blessed Virgin

1. To all those who shall recite my Rosary devoutly, I promise my special protection and very great graces.

2. Those who shall persevere in the recitation of my Rosary will receive some signal grace.

3. The Rosary will be a very powerful armor against hell; it will destroy vice, deliver from sin, and dispel heresy.

4. The Rosary will make virtue and good works flourish, and will obtain for souls the most abundant divine mercies; it will substitute in hearts love of God for love of the world, and elevate them to desire heavenly and eternal goods. Oh, that souls would sanctify themselves by this means!

5. Those who trust themselves to me through the Rosary will not perish.

6. Those who shall recite my Rosary piously, considering its mysteries, will not be overwhelmed by misfortune, nor die a bad death.

7. Those truly devoted to my Rosary shall not die without the consolations of the Church or without grace.

8. Those who shall recite my Rosary will find during their life and at their death the light of God, the fullness of His grace, and will share in the merits of the blessed.

9. I will deliver very promptly from purgatory the souls devoted to my Rosary.

10. The true children of my Rosary will enjoy great glory in heaven.

11. What you shall ask through my Rosary you shall obtain.

12. Those who propagate my Rosary will obtain through me aid in all their necessities.

13. I have obtained from my Son that all the members of the Rosary Confraternity shall have for their intercessors in life and death the saints of heaven.

14. Those who recite my Rosary faithfully are all my beloved children, the brothers and sisters of Jesus Christ.

15. Devotion to my Rosary is a special sign of predestination.

(The foregoing promises were made to St. Dominic and Blessed Alan in favor of those devoted to the Blessed Mother's Rosary.)